RYAN IS READY FOR YOU NOW...

The insider's guide to interviewing a celebrity – from a journalist who was in the room

By

Lisa Marks

ISBN:978-1-5272-7120-3

First Edition

September 2020

“Care for a nut?”
Cate Blanchett, the Beverly Wilshire, Los Angeles,
2007

DEDICATION

For David Marks and Howard Delmonte. The real celebrities in my life.

PREFACE

Welcome to *Ryan Is Ready For You Now…*, a collection of stories, anecdotes, and insights from my 30 years as a celebrity journalist.

Before I sat down in front of my trusty laptop with the now invisible 'A' key, I had to ask myself why I wanted to spend a ridiculous amount of time sequestered by myself, and going slightly mad, writing a book about my career interviewing (mainly) the rich and the famous.

I knew I wanted to tell a good story. Good storytelling is the reason I do what I do, and I have plenty of them to tell. I'm also asked constantly about the celebrities I've interviewed, so I know that the fascination is endless. Friends, family, and strangers ask me to tell them the same stories again and again.

Now because of this book I don't have to; they can keep this tome on their bedside table, or tablet, and guffaw at the time I sang a show tune at Hugh Jackman, sobbed on Drew Barrymore's shoulder or tucked into Scarlett Johansson's trail mix, without having me physically in the room.

In an act of great hubris, I also feel compelled to pass on a few tricks of the trade and do my bit for an industry that I love. It's one that's taken more than a few knocks recently.

I think it's useful stuff, it's filling up my head and frankly, I need to put it somewhere. Also, a book – a book! - is a natural next step for a journo of a certain vintage and also to be fair, some form of therapy, so do be kind.

As well as putting in my years as a news reporter, feature writer, columnist, commissioning editor, showbiz editor, launch editor, and all around interviewer extraordinaire, I've been a visiting lecturer in Journalism at Oxford Brookes University, the University of Winchester, and a part-time lecturer in magazine journalism at the University of Gloucestershire. It appears that I'm now at an age where peering over the top of my reading glasses and imparting useful nuggets of information has become as satisfying as interesting conversation over a whisky cocktail in a quiet bar followed by a decent night's sleep.

I'm also a media coach helping others navigate the world of celebrity interviews, A-list junkets, and on-camera chit-chat. It sounds glamorous, but it's usually either very cold or very hot so wear layers. Please consider that my first tip.

What's utterly mind-blowing if I think about it too long is how the media, and the way we digest our news, has changed beyond recognition since I joined a local paper in the late eighties.

Fortunately, when it comes to interviewing celebrities, the essence of what I do has remained the same: meet famous person, try to get something interesting out of famous person, then write, edit, or produce something that people will want to read, listen to, or watch.

A journalist exists to inform, educate, and entertain. This triangle of goodness will never change and whether you now choose to read an actual physical newspaper or magazine, or soak up content on your watch, phone, or tablet, the same stands for all.

This book will tell you how to go about doing a good job of something that everyone thinks they can do, but few can do well.

And you want to do it well, don't you?

I also wrote this book to prove I could. I enjoy long-form journalism, and this is as long-form as it gets. Although as I reach the end of the process, I honestly feel like I've been writing this book since before the invention of paper.

Yet still my idea of journo heaven remains a chunky magazine assignment following around [insert name of fabulous yet slightly reclusive and/or intriguing famous person] for days, including a few days on their yacht just for the hell of it, with 5,000 words to deliver on completion of our time together. I live in hope.

So, settle down and prepare to join me in a lifetime of journalistic derring-do, discovery, and delight. If you love Hollywood, showbusiness, and celebrities I hope you'll be thoroughly entertained by the stories that follow, and if this is your chosen path, my wish is that it will inspire you in some tangible way.

I hope you enjoy the book and if you do, please let me know by emailing lisamarksmedia@gmail.com or by following me on Twitter @lisamarks.

Let's get on with it.

Lisa Marks

AUTHOR'S NOTE

Throughout this book I describe actual interview situations I've encountered to illustrate the realities of working in this industry. These are my stories, my anecdotes, my opinions, and my experiences. In most of these instances, I've named the celebrity or celebrities involved. These are the people who I've met over the last 30 years through my work, they are the reason this book exists and the reason my byline has been seen in so many publications. I thank them for that.

While this book is on one hand a memoir of my life as a media professional covering the entertainment industry, it's also designed to be an informative teaching tool for anyone setting out on the same path. No stories are told with malice. Every anecdote relates to a lesson that could be learnt.

The stories are not based upon blind gossip. It was important for me to be as transparent as I could where possible and use real names. Many of my interviews are available online, and it would be easy to join the dots if you were looking to discover anyone I've been cryptic about. To hide identities would have been futile.

Where I haven't named names, it is for either legal reasons, or because I decided that to name that person would either be too great a breach of privacy or an embarrassment to that person to do so. In all, I've tried to keep the anonymous anecdotes to a minimum.

INTRODUCTION

I interviewed my first bona fide celebrity in 1988. I was a reporter on the *Southend Evening Echo*, in Essex, and was sent to an independent record store in the centre of town to meet Donny Osmond.

That's where my celebrity-interviewing career started and I shall return to this meeting a little later because there were lessons to be learnt, and also to give anyone under the age of 40 the chance to Google the name Donny Osmond.

I'm going to start this book in 2007, the year I relocated from London to Los Angeles to cover the entertainment industry.

Hollywood was calling and I attended more press junkets, red carpets, press conferences, and roundtables during my time in LA than at any other point in my career.

It was an exciting few years, but I was repeatedly told two things before that giant leap across the pond:

- You won't make any real friends because no one makes real friends in LA.

- You're going to get shot.

Fortunately, neither proved true.

What the proverbial 'they' should have said was that two things will happen to you when you move to Los Angeles:

1. Without putting in any effort whatsoever, your British accent will open doors for you and lull people into thinking you're more intelligent than you actually are.
2. You will come to learn that in a town where youth, beauty, and box office hits are the benchmark of success, the day that the head valet at the Four Seasons Hotel, in Beverly Hills, greets you by name as you check in at yet another international press junket, that you've come as close as you ever will to 'making it'. Surprisingly, you will be very happy about this.

Once I moved to LA to interview the stars, the questions duly changed, but two were repeated more times than most.

1. Is that a British accent? (A daily occurrence)

2. What's Ryan Gosling like? (An almost daily occurrence).

The first is obviously yes, it is a British accent. I was born in St Theresa's Hospital, Wimbledon, London, on July 15th, 1968.

It's rare for a woman to tell the world her real age, and I think, actually illegal in Hollywood. Call this my rebellion or call it mere stupidity. These are the numbers, and I'm stuck with them. May as well 'fess up and be thought of as brave for telling the truth. And while, now and again, I may shave a year or two off, frankly, I'm proud to have been born in the same year as the Beatles' *White Album*.

Despite my mum's frantic worries that I might lose my polite-but-ever-so-slightly broad Thames Estuary accent, I began to sound more British during my time in Los Angeles. In an attempt to stave off any kind of hybrid British-American twang, I went from Essex-girl-turned-London-journo to Kensington Palace-posh, skirting the fringes of the BBC circa 1957.

Side note: *Only when ordering food in an American diner, should you take the vintage royal tones down a notch. Water will soon become 'wadder', or believe me, you will spend ten minutes trying to make your server understand this simple request. And who wants to spend ten minutes ordering water when you can be eating a stack of pancakes taller than Chewbacca?*

A British accent in America is vocal gold. It ascribes you kudos, insight, and a certain air of mystery that no one should ever deserve. I loved it. It got me into bars and events, and out of many scrapes, including a couple of parking tickets.

But as for the second question, the answer was always: "Sorry, I don't know what Ryan Gosling is like. I've never met him."

Their face would fall, and I'd chime in with: "But I've interviewed Keanu Reeves. *The Matrix*! *Bill and Ted*!" Minor interest. A mention of 007 Daniel Craig would ironically invoke half a raised eyebrow. Jennifer Aniston might elicit a curious: "Ooooh, was she nice?" but my celebrity name-drops never seemed gold-standard Gosling enough.

Ryan's sleeper hit, *Half Nelson*, had come out the year before I moved to LA, and almost from the moment I landed, his star was in ascendance. Back then Jake Gyllenhaal was the 'it' man, but within a matter of months Jake, a most excellent actor, seemed like yesterday's news. It had to be Gosling.

To coin a hackneyed phrase, there's something about Ryan. Young women love him, older women adore him, and even women who are so old they can remember food rationing feel warm and fuzzy at the sight of him. And it's not just women; men, children, and babies love him too. The guy is essentially human pizza. Hell, if you look on YouTube, there's probably a cat swooning on the carpet in front of one of his movies.

I could take three Charlize Therons, add a sprinkling of Harrison Ford, and a layer of Cameron Diaz (and I did all of that, of which more later), and I still wouldn't have enough meat in my Hollywood sandwich. The filling had to be Gosling.

I use the sandwich analogy because it's ridiculous, and also because Americans love their sandwiches. Once you've devoured a corned beef on rye with a side of slaw and potato salad from an authentic American deli, your heart will tell you that the meagre British equivalent will never cut the mustard.

Side note: *their mustard is rubbish, always carry a jar of Colman's, and if you're really thinking ahead, a bottle of Sarson's malt vinegar as Americans don't do vinegar on their chips. I kept a bottle in the boot of my car the entire time I lived there.*

This may sound pedantic, but it's a huge fallacy that people in Los Angeles don't eat. They eat a lot and all the time. Food is often the subject of a conversation and I became a bona fide ex-pat foodie. I would drive hours across town for the best pork belly sandwich (Forage, in Silverlake, who have sadly now taken it off their menu goddammit), the most luscious burrito (steak chipotle at Hugo's, in Atwater Village), or the most succulent burger (Sunny Spot, in Venice Beach, when it was owned by the fabulous Roy Choi).

And don't get me started on the oysters from Morro Bay. Actually, really don't. I went to Morro Bay in central California once, and sadly, never got to try any. But I hear they're fantastic.

So, Gosling. The holy grail of all interviewees. It was a question I had to live with daily, and I often wondered if it would ever happen. Would I be lucky enough to sit in a room with the man who turns the world to jelly/jello? Could the actor whose movie credits included *Blue Valentine*, *Drive*, *The Notebook*, *The Ides of March*, *Crazy, Stupid, Love*, *Gangster Squad*, *La La Land*, and *Blade Runner 2049* be a featured artist in my own Hollywood odyssey?

First, I had to find my feet. I'd only been to LA twice before I relocated there.

The first time was on a press trip when I was working for UK teen mag *BIG!* in 1994. It was during the World Cup, but nobody on the West Coast gave two hoots about that. Pre-David Beckham and pre pre-Landon Donovan, football in the States was largely ignored.

Oddly, most of the Americans I met played football – or soccer as they call it – at junior school, but by the time they got to college, it was all about the NFL. Soccer was forgotten. Shoulder pads, quarterbacks, and cheerleaders ruled the roost.

My press trip was courtesy of Disney to celebrate the release of *Aladdin* on video. Now there's an easy way to age yourself in one short sentence.

Our home for the trip was the Sheraton Universal Hotel, in Studio City, overlooking what I know now as the fragrant 101 freeway. I almost didn't make it as I was separated from my group by the TSA at LAX airport for having a fresh plum in my handbag. I watched as they threw this utterly harmless yet hugely offensive fruit into a furnace, and it was only after a curt telling-off that I was allowed to proceed to the arrivals hall.

Jet-lagged to the hilt on my first morning, I staggered into the lift with three other chaps. Through my lag I pulled focus to see that I was standing next to Terry Venables, Jim Rosenthal, and Jimmy Hill, who were there to commentate on the footie. It was as close to a sporting dream sequence as you'll ever get. My dad knew Terry in the sixties (and would pop over for tea and cake at Terry's aunt's), so I caught up with the then England coach later in the hotel bar for a chat which was lovely.

The second time I visited California was in 2006, when I visited an old school friend and her family. As soon as I landed, I knew I wanted to spend more time there. I was ready. It took a while, but I got my visa sponsorship through *The Guardian* who I was working for at the time on the Media pages, chucked almost everything I owned into storage and threw a goodbye party.

Two suitcases full of bikinis and shorts later, I landed at LAX on January 31 2007 to freezing cold weather. I immediately made my friend drive me to the mall to buy practical clothes that would actually keep me warm.

Here's another Hollywood myth; it's not always hot. It rains more than you think and because of the desert micro-climate once the sun goes down it's chilly at night. But generally, who am I kidding, it's warm and sunny.

I loved it. I'd been a journalist in London for 15 years working on magazines and newspapers, but I'd also sold a couple of movie scripts. I figured, if I was going to live anywhere else, it had to be where I could work as a film and entertainment journalist, and also maybe have a shot at selling a movie script.

My LA Diary ran in the *Guardian Film Blog* pages for almost two years, charting my writing and film-making adventures. I won a film competition and shot my first short in New Mexico in 2007, was twice a quarter-finalist in the prestigious Academy Nicholl Fellowships in Screenwriting, and signed a couple of deal memos. Not exactly Oscar-winning, but not too shabby either.

In the meantime, to earn a crust I became a regular on the movie junket circuit working for among others, *The Guardian*, *The Scotsman,* and the *Sunday Telegraph* in Sydney, and the *Sunday Herald-Sun* in Victoria, Australia (from now on referred to as *Sunday Magazine*).

Junket isn't a term that many people recognise. It sounds like a character from *Breaking Bad* but it's actually the word movie studios use for gathering their top line talent in one place and bringing in the Hollywood foreign and domestic press, for a happy little exchange that will hopefully boost their film's chances at the box office.

You put on smart clothes, drive an hour across LA (it's always an hour no matter what), valet your car at a swanky hotel, wander around for a while until you find the correct suite/floor, check in with the studio publicist, help yourself to the free food in hospitality, and wait to be called into a usually overwarm room. You will then spend ten, 20, or if you're lucky, 30 to 40 precious minutes of face time with an A-lister, who is, truth be told, bored senseless from answering the same questions for 48 hours straight.

This is where the skill comes in. Press junkets are a production line, a sausage machine for spoiled journalists, who will walk into a hospitality room filled to the rafters with exquisite snacks and exclaim, "This is a travesty, why isn't there any chicken parmigiana?"

I saw a lot, I heard a lot, and I learnt a lot. And – teaser alert! – I'm going to tell you more about all of it in the coming chapters.

Los Angeles was a new start, a fresh place to call home and as I soon realised from the constant enquiries, my hunting ground for Ryan.

I stood in line for coffee with Jennifer Aniston, nodded to Leonardo DiCaprio at the traffic lights, waved at Jamie Foxx on the freeway and watched in awe as Elijah Wood cycled past me in Venice balancing a pizza box on the handlebars of his bike. Gosling was out there somewhere. He had to be because I wanted to be able to say to inquiring minds, "Yes, I have met Ryan Gosling. He was short." Or tall? Whimsical? Giggly? Smelling of peanuts? Made of unicorn hair? Indeed, anything that was anecdotally sufficient to silence my inquisitors.

I was ready for him. Little did I realise it would take a while. They say there's no such thing as overnight success in Hollywood, and boy, were they right.

But that was okay because I had a few more famous people to speak to first, copy to write, and Hollywood to conquer.

You may never get to Los Angeles, but that's okay because it's not compulsory. This book covers my entire career on both sides of the Atlantic. It's my blueprint for the job, and it's the same job whether you're interviewing an A-lister in Malibu or a reality star in Brentwood, Essex. This is my manifesto and my point of view. You will most likely decide to do things differently and of course, that's absolutely fine because no one way is the right way.

A friend once told me that to work in Hollywood you have to be extraordinary because the best of the best work there. And so, in 2007, I found myself working at the most extraordinary level and although at times it was terrifying, I loved it.

Everything I'd learnt up to that point in my career came into play, but I made it my mission to soak up everything around me and then do better. I had to. I had to keep up. I was now part of the Hollywood publicity machine. It was as far from meeting Donny Osmond in a record shop in Southend-on-Sea as I could possibly get. And that meant I had to be nearer Ryan, right?

All I needed to do was not get shot, make new friends, and learn the name of every hotel valet in town.

Any questions?

CHAPTER ONE

WHY ARE YOU IN THE ROOM?

I've always had a keen celebrity radar.

I can move through a crowd and unconsciously find a famous face even when I'm not searching for one.

It's a skill of sorts, this celebrity *Where's Wally*? of mine. Granted, it's not as useful as knowing CPR but for me it's more useful than say, being able to make a pyramid out of a deck of playing cards or a swan out of a napkin.

It's not an obsession, more a fascination. I'm curious about everyone, not just the names we all recognise, and oddly, that hasn't changed over the years. There's always more to learn and more to discover.

But there's an undeniable allure to celebrity, and for some reason my career path has always delivered me to their gold-plated door and also their silver crushed-velvet sofas (a reality star staple).

But what is the nature of celebrity? How are celebrities different from us? Are they different? Do they deserve our adulation? Our time? I might be able to answer some of that but one thing I know for sure is that growing up, celebrity was treated in very different ways in the Marks family household.

My parents covered both extremes. My dad, David, a businessman, had celebrity friends and was also an after-dinner speaker, musician, and former stand-up. His best friend was the late England goalie Peter Bonetti, and hanging around Chelsea FC and the England team in the sixties and seventies, Dad had plenty of opportunity to mix in showbiz circles. He loved it.

As well as football, he was such a film buff that aside from the lead actors, he could generally name the extras and bit players in any movie or TV show we watched together. Or at least that's how it seemed to young me.

Memorably, he would make my brother and I name the actors who played *The Magnificent Seven* (the original movie) before we sat down to eat Sunday lunch. All I'll say to you is 'Brad Dexter'. People always forget poor Brad.

On the other hand, my mother, Barbara (from now on known as Babs), had zero interest in the celebrity world. I once asked her who was her favourite actor and after what seemed like a week, and also a mini lecture on how she didn't really care, she came up with the name Patrick McGoohan.

This was sometime in the noughties and Patrick McGoohan was famous for his lead role in the sixties TV series *The Prisoner*. It was a left field choice, but there you go, that's Babs.

While I was living in Hollywood, Babs came to visit. I was living at that time near the CBS Studios and had just interviewed an Australian dancer called Kym Johnson, who was one of the professionals on the show *Dancing with the Stars*, which is the US version of *Strictly Come Dancing*.

I told Kym that Mum was a big fan of the show in the UK, so she arranged for me to have two tickets to the live show that weekend. Thankfully, and despite the fact that Patrick McGoohan wasn't in the cast that year, Mum was thrilled.

We put our posh dresses on and walked five minutes up the road to the studios. I'd borrowed a dress from a stylist friend without asking, thinking I would wear it, Febreze it, and put it back into its bag without her noticing. My plan spectacularly backfired when the studio manager, for no apparent reason, placed Mum and me on a prominent two-seater row, which was square on camera, at the spot where the dancers made their entrance onto the floor. I was so squirmy throughout the taping I may as well have been wearing a 40-foot sign that said, *I'm a terrible person, I borrowed this dress without permission*!

It had been left in my apartment after a photo shoot for safe-keeping and there it was, plastered all over primetime network television in glorious Technicolor.

We were also seated near to some of the celebrity dancers' families, by the stairs which swooped the couples up towards the balcony for their post-dance debrief.

Mum recognised Ricki Lake (hurrah!) and waved at her. Ricki waved back (also hurrah!). Kym came over to say hello. The cast also included original *Queer Eye* cast member Carson Kressley, Chaz Bono, Chynna Phillips, David Arquette, and Rob Kardashian. Yes, a Kardashian. What that meant in practical terms was that a handful of members from one of the most famous families on earth, the Kardashians, were sitting in front of us. I remember that night seeing Kim, her sisters, and their mum Kris Jenner (more of the world's most famous 'momager' later) grouped together.

After the taping, which went on for around five (hundred) hours, including two rounds of Susan Boyle pre-recording a performance of her latest single for the following week's show, we were released from our seats.

Cue the stampede for the toilets.

In the post-show melee, I stepped away from Mum to talk to someone I knew and when I turned back, I saw that Babs was deep in conversation with Kim Kardashian. Ha.

Mum is five foot nothing and the first thing I noticed was that she and Kim were the same height.

I watched in amusement as they chatted like old pals. After they exchanged goodbyes, Mum walked back to me and said with no sense of occasion, "I've just been speaking to a lovely girl called Kimberly."

Kimberly.

I'll just let that sit there.

It amuses me to this day that the woman who has 183 million (and counting) followers on Instagram, introduced herself to my mum as Kimberly. It was very sweet.

I replied, "Do you have any idea who she is?"

"No," said Babs. And she didn't ask.

That's how uninterested in celebrity my mum is. She couldn't even recognise Kim Kardashian when Kim, standing less than two feet away, formally introduced herself to my mother, in person, using her own name.

On another memorable occasion I left Babs to her own devices to have a mani/pedi at a salon in Santa Monica, and when I arrived to pick her up, she was hugging an exceptionally gorgeous woman goodbye.

"Bye, Mena, nice to meet you!" said Babs breezily.

It was actress Mena Suvari, the star of *American Beauty*, and again Mum had absolutely no idea who she was. When I told her again she was utterly unimpressed, noting that she was a "nice girl" and that they'd had a lovely chat.

Celebrity. It's intoxicating for most. Just not for Babs.

But while Mum may not be able to understand the world's fascination, the interest in celebrity is by no means lessening as time goes on.

People have always been attracted to the lives of rich, attractive, successful, long-limbed, beautiful people, and the rise of social media has merely fuelled the flames of this mania. The more we're allowed tantalising glimpses into their lives, the more, it seems, we want to know.

There may not be the same kind of studio-controlled mystery as there was back in the days of Richard Burton and Elizabeth Taylor, but in my experience there's always more to learn if you're allowed the opportunity to dig a little deeper.

Social media has diluted the mystery somewhat, but celebrities are like us. At least that's what they want us to think, and every brand depends on an authentic connection. Opening the doors to their private lives, and their kitchens and bedrooms, has given famous faces an unfiltered voice they never had before. It has enabled them to express themselves without the aid of a publicist (and most likely given their publicists' daily anxiety attacks as they veer dangerously off message). I think celebrities today tread a narrow path between inviting us into their private lives online and revealing any inner thoughts that could lead to a social media pile on.

I'm certain that if movie stars from the vintage era were at their peak today, they too would be tweeting about their oat milk latte or posing in their underwear in front of the mirror in their bathrooms. In this day and age, it's what's expected, but at the same time celebrities are also aware of their reach and how their social media platform can be used for good.

However, social media has made life a little more difficult for the celebrity profiler who is searching for quality access. The market is saturated with content and most of it has been recycled and rehashed. There are numerous magazines and websites that simply cut and paste whatever a celebrity has said on Twitter that day and pass it off as a news story, along with all the accompanying cheeky emojis, hashtags, and spelling mistakes.

This kind of filler is quick to churn out, but it's pure click bait serving only to promote a stampede of traffic to whatever site you're reading. The upside is that it creates jobs, thanks to lucrative advertising revenue, but it's not journalism. Describing a set of photos is lazy. End of.

Ultimately, for a writer who cares about the words and the story, and who is there to really get to know more about their subject, the job to fight past the surface noise is harder than ever. You have to be really good at what you do to profile a celebrity and discover something new. Thankfully, I'm here to help you with that (cheeky wink emoji #interviewskillz).

The flipside of this publishing revolution is that everyone with a blog and an Instagram account thinks they can be a journalist, and many more think they should also be a celebrity. Yes, technically, anyone can be a celebrity. But if you're a journalist who thinks it's your job to be a celebrity like the people you're interviewing, then think again.

That is not your job. If you want to be a celebrity, do it. Knock yourself out.

On occasion, journalists end up being a part of the story but they're still not *the* celebrity. You may be labouring under the illusion of living a celebrity lifestyle as you 'rock up' to a five-star hotel in your smart outfit before being whisked to the penthouse suite for an audience with an uber famous A-lister but if you're being sent to do an interview, then you are absolutely not the focus and you are not the story.

Showbusiness is an intoxicating world, so I understand the desire that people have to inhabit that world too.

But it's a strange place to live. Hell, even celebrities find celebrity odd. I remember Christina Hendricks sharing this nugget during an interview in August 2008: "January Jones told me she was at a party and Mariah Carey was there being followed by her people with a CD player with her album playing on it. What if I had people following me around with a TV with *Mad Men* playing on a loop? That would be so amazing! I think people do these things because they know it'll get attention, even if it's ridiculous."

Being in awe of a celebrity or wanting to be a celebrity is not what's required to be a really good celebrity interviewer.

Star power can have a strange effect on people, and there have been times when I've been overawed in the company of someone famous. Dame Julie Andrews springs to mind because she's a bona fide legend and was everything I wanted her to be and a spoonful more. I've gushed endlessly to friends about various encounters with famous people and have witnessed, and sometimes experienced, the rarefied air they breathe and enjoyed a taste of their luxury lifestyles. Just a toe dip, but enough to understand why someone would want to be a celebrity with all the trappings. The allure of their world is truly magnetic. The celebrities themselves are usually charismatic and in many ways beguiling. There's a pull and a power, and many times it's utterly inexplicable. It just is.

One of the most visceral experiences of 'star power' I can recall was at an event thrown by the Director's Guild of America, in Los Angeles, ahead of the release of *The Kennedys* mini-series, in 2011.

Actress Katie Holmes, then Tom Cruise's wife, played Jackie Kennedy, and was expected to attend, as was Barry Pepper, who played Robert Kennedy. Tom was not scheduled to be at the screening, for which I recall there was an unusually high level of security.

I remember taking my seat in the audience and was busy people watching before the lights went down. The place slowly filled up and the noise level was the usual hubbub before a screening.

Everything was normal until suddenly it wasn't.

The hairs on the back of my neck stood up. The atmosphere in the room, a large theatre, changed in a split second. There was a hush, a frisson, an excitement.

I turned around, curious to find out what had caused this surge of electricity just in time to see Katie Holmes walking towards her seat accompanied by Tom Cruise. There he was, the star of *Mission: Impossible*, and all the other *Mission: Impossibles* that followed.

Tom's presence changed the energy in the room, and he didn't have to enter suspended from the ceiling to do it.

In the many hundreds of interviews I've done and the unbelievably famous people I've met or been in close proximity to, I have never, ever seen an individual have that effect on a roomful of people. Nothing close. And these were mostly industry people; people who lived in a movie-making town and were used to being around stars, not fizzy teenagers who fainted at the sight of a signed copy of *Twilight*. It was incredible.

Fan or not, that man exuded a mega-wattage charisma. It was unassailable raw star power and it was compelling.

I spent most of the screening looking at the back of Tom's head. I admit, it was weird. Not his head – that ticked all the regular requirements for a head – but the effect his presence had on me and literally everyone else in that room.

I've never interviewed Tom Cruise in a one-to-one situation, a group, or press conference. I don't know him at all. I know he's a Scientologist and I know who he's been married to and the names of his children. Professionally, I've heard that he always brings his A game and that he's charming in interviews. He also follows me on Twitter, so he's obviously hugely discerning. But that's it.

So that entire episode was odd but – and this is most likely Mum's influence – in general, I'm not one for hero worship and I think it helps to have that distance in an interview situation.

Journalists must be objective. It's the only way to do the job properly. You must never forget that being a celebrity is a business. Keep it front and centre that the person you're talking to is a money-maker. They are making money for themselves, their managers, publicists, studio, record company, publishers, stylists, families, production companies. The list goes on and on.

At their core they're a commodity, part of a giant machine whose wheels must keep on turning no matter what. Livings and lifestyles depend on it. The same goes for the media company you're working for too. You are making money for them. That's it.

The minute you step into the room you become part of that machine. And if you're lucky enough to be in the room, and by that I mean in a one-to-one interview situation, at a roundtable, press conference, on the red carpet or any other kind of press junket, and you haven't come to engage and do your job, then I question your motive for being there in the first place.

You are a key part of why this all works, and you need to do what is expected of you. I realise this sounds cynical but believe me when I say that I'm not cold-hearted about celebrity. As I edit this intro before publication, I'm watching David Bowie's 2000 Glastonbury set on BBC2 during the Covid-19 lockdown. It was an immense performance. Bowie, who died in 2016, was an extraordinary artist, connector, teacher, and innovator. I didn't truly find his music until I was well into my thirties, but when I did it became an integral part of my life. That being said, if I'd had the good fortune to interview him before he passed away, it would still have been 95% business with a smidge of fangirl thrown in for geeky good measure.

Know that, first and foremost, you are in the room to ask questions, record the answers, write good stories, and provide great content. In fact, that's all you're there to do. But doing it well takes skill, practice, and application. You cannot be swayed from the job at hand by having stars in your eyes. The machine will not stop for gooey eyed you.

It sounds harsh, but most people only see the end product of celebrity and showbusiness, the designer dresses, the power, and the glamour. But the work that it takes to keep that person there is something completely different.

Business is business and work is work, and you are there to work.

That's not to say that I haven't been thrown off-guard by various situations in the past. There has been the odd time or two when I've not done my job properly. Not because I wanted to be the star but because the star, in my opinion, did not do their job or hold up their end of the bargain.

In the interests of fairness I have to hold my hand up and admit to there being one time I was so mad at an A-lister at a movie junket, I literally couldn't speak to ask a question.

I'd been flown from Los Angeles to New Orleans to interview Brucc Willis on the set of the 2010 action movie *RED*. His co-stars, who were also on set that day, were John Malkovich, Mary-Louise Parker, and Karl Urban.

Set visits are usually a lot of fun; they are a glimpse behind the great Oz curtain of Hollywood. They always zip by in a flash, but while you're there, you get to see the detailed process of movie-making up close, and you also get to eat craft services. Do not underestimate how good movie set food is. Think of the last great meal your mum cooked and then elevate it to Christmas dinner proportions and then times it by a thousand. Maybe I love it so much because I love anyone who cooks for me, but I'm always excited when breakfast, lunchtime, afternoon snack, or dinner time rolls around on set.

The location for this particular visit was ridiculously memorable. We were driven on the first morning of our two-day stay from our hotel, which was near to Decatur Street in the French District of the city, to the Port of New Orleans. The port is the sixth largest in the States, has a two-mile-long wharf, and handles around 60 million tons of cargo a year. It's big.

Arriving on location in the blistering heat (this detail will become key later in the story) our merry little press gang (I think there were around ten of us) were told that we'd be watching an action sequence being filmed and after that we would be interviewing the cast.

Here are the notes from my archives:

1. You will be observing an exciting action scene filmed on location (not in studio).
2. The sequence includes:
    a. A mysterious businesswoman who fires at Marvin (Malkovich)
    b. A rooftop sniper erupts in gunfire
    c. Businesswoman fires rocket
    d. Frank (Willis) and Marvin return fire
    e. Scissor-lift explodes like a toy
    f. Marvin fires at the rocket detonating it.

Exciting movie stuff! A fork-lift truck literally exploded in front of us. We were at a safe distance and wearing goggles but even so, we could feel the heat from the flames, which were quickly extinguished.

After all that excitement, we were taken to a small area where we were told to wait under a canopy for Bruce. The set up here was the same as if we were at a roundtable in a hotel; this is where journalists sit around a table and *lo!* a celebrity appears as if by magic and everyone gets the chance to interview them in a group setting.

The heat was still blistering, and the canopy was useless in terms of keeping us cool. But we waited. And we waited. And we waited. We waited a really long time.

Word on set was that Bruce didn't, for whatever reason, want to leave his trailer. I don't know why. I don't know if it was us or something else, but there was little that we or the publicists and assistants could do.

John Malkovich wandered over to talk to us, which in all fairness was pretty bloody brilliant. If that man ever starts a cult, I'm in. Words escape his mouth like caramel-covered poetry. Enjoying holding court, he sat with us for an hour or so. Lovely man and a wonderful experience.

Still no Bruce.

A while later we were led away from the canopy to another bigger canopy that served as craft services. Fried chicken, mac and cheese, giant bowls of colourful salads and enormous fruit platters spread out before us. We ate a hearty meal and after lunch were taken back to the press area. Surrounded by looming steel containers, we were carefully watched over by security. The afternoon sun blazed down from a clear, blue sky and the temperature was insufferable. The ground absorbed all the heat and smacked it back into our sweaty faces. There was nowhere to escape. Everyone was wilting.

We spoke to Mary-Louise Parker and Karl Urban. Mary-Louise Parker was personable as was Karl Urban, a New Zealand-born actor, who talked about his role as Doctor 'Bones' McCoy in the recently rebooted *Star Trek* franchise.

No Bruce. No Bruce. No Bruce. Heat. No Bruce. Thirsty. No Bruce. Irritable.

No Bruce. Really, really hot. Headache. No Bruce. Dehydrating. No Bruce. Now getting extremely grumpy. Headache worse.

No Bruce.

Suddenly, Bruce.

My brief for *the Sunday Telegraph* was to get a Bruce Willis interview, and Bruce only. None of the other interviews had been any use to me in terms of print, only in terms of personal excitement and colour.

When I'd been asked to join the trip, I was thrilled because not only had I never been to New Orleans (which I loved) but I was a genuine Bruce Willis fan and had been since his days on the TV show *Moonlighting*. A comedy/drama, it first appeared on our screens a couple of years before I joined the local newspaper and there was something about the irreverence of Bruce Willis's character, David Addison, and his relationship with Cybill Shepherd's character, Maddie Hayes, that reminded me of the tight-knit team I worked with on the *Evening Echo*. Then when *Die Hard* came out in 1988, Bruce went from TV star to global superstar. Levels of fame, that's another subject of fascination.

So, much later than planned, he sauntered over to our table, grinned in an exceptionally cheeky manner, sat in the one empty chair in the middle of the table, leaned back, spread his legs, pointed his finger at me and said, "Question." Just like that.

I froze. I literally couldn't speak because I was so hot, so headachy, so uncomfortable, and let's face it, so angry. Some may call his actions movie star charisma, some may not.

He quickly moved on to another journalist. I know I fell short, but the interview turned out okay. He answered everyone's questions and was funny. Everyone laughed heartily, which always helps make an interview situation less awkward. Again, as with every A-lister when they turn on the charm, it's like that zapping device they use in the movie *Men in Black* where you forget everything that's gone before.

For me personally though it was a big Yippee ki-no in terms of assignment satisfaction.

After Bruce disappeared, the publicist asked why I hadn't asked a question and I told her it was because I was feeling unwell, which was at least true. The heat had made me queasy and brought on a headache, but it wasn't that alone. I was so mad at him for keeping us waiting all day and then behaving like it was nothing when he eventually turned up that words were unable to escape from my lips.

Later, back at the hotel, I beat myself up over my stroppy reaction. Mostly, I was upset was because I didn't do my best.

I'm telling you this story because this is probably as bad as it got in terms of me not showing up in the room. It doesn't matter how hot it was or why Bruce kept us waiting or what I was feeling personally, I was still there to do a job.

Using the questions from the roundtable, the interview turned out fine. My intro to the story that was eventually published starts with the words "Bruce Willis is upbeat" which made me laugh when I read it back while doing research for this chapter.

Let's be clear, I've never failed to deliver a piece of work to length and on time. But on that day, I believe that I failed, and I do not want you to fail.

It wasn't the end of the world, but I will say this, you should always treat people with respect. No matter who you are, what side of the camera you're on, or how big an artist you are, there is no reason to behave badly. I know it's terribly old fashioned of me, but good manners will reward you time and again in this job.

I was lucky to have been asked on that trip, and I'm still annoyed with myself all these years later at not being able to utter one question through my very British non-hissy, hissy fit.

Curiosity is the fundamental drive for every journalist. You simply have to know more. I shouldn't have been swayed by circumstance and it never happened again no matter how tricky the customer was. And as for Bruce Willis, chances are, in another situation, he would have been timely and I'd have thrown a hundred questions his way. But on that day, he wasn't and that was my experience. It's a good reminder that you shouldn't have high expectations of one person. Just do the job.

So, to Cristelle, the publicist who was on set with us that day in New Orleans, I apologise.

To the rest of you, let's get on with the nuts and bolts of interviewing a celebrity. The wheels of this machine need to keep moving.

HEADLINES:

When you're in the room, you're there to do a job.
You're not there to make a friend.
Do your best, even when others are not.
Celebrity is intoxicating, stay focused.
Celebrity is infuriating, stay focused.

CHAPTER TWO

DECIPHERING YOUR BRIEF

The words 'celebrity' and 'briefs' probably conjure up images of David Beckham or Freddie Ljungberg in a pair of bulging tighty-whities. Sorry to disappoint but this chapter isn't about underwear or the celebrity real estate they cover (although some might call what I've written here a load of old balls). Nope, this is about something very different indeed.

Before you meet any celebrity and willfully stick a recording device under their nose or a camera in their face, you need to know why you're there, what's required from the interview, how long the piece should be and your deadline.

This useful information won't just fall out of the sky. The person hiring or commissioning you will supply you with a brief which is the blueprint for your assignment. Ignore it at your peril. At this point, you should also negotiate your fee.

Briefs are essential to the process but to be honest, they're not always as good as they should be. Because of this, you need to have your wits about you.

A scrappy brief is the disappointing equivalent of getting socks as a Christmas present. It may have been bashed out last minute or maybe the editor sending it is simply no good at writing them. Maybe they just don't care (avoid these people where possible).

Worse than a scrappy brief is a wishy-washy one. Like a disappointing first date, you so want it to be good and when it's not you know that you have an awkward, uphill climb ahead of you.

However, if you stumble across a commissioning editor who can write a succinct, informative brief, you've struck gold. Send them flowers on their birthday and tell them constantly how much you love them.

When I was a commissioning editor on the *Daily Mirror's* TV magazine, *The Look*, in the early noughties, I made it my mission to write detailed yet concise briefs. I sent the briefs I wanted sent to me and found that it was always worth my while spending a little extra time outlining what I needed because when I did that, I got the copy I required.

When I left *The Mirror,* one of my regular freelancers emailed to say she would miss my briefs (note not me, just my briefs!).

There's nothing worse than getting a brief that says We need around 1,000 to 3000-ish words, more or less, maybe along the lines of their love of smoothies, swimming, or Ryan Gosling, or whatever will fill a page, with an intro and three pull quotes but don't worry if you don't have time and send it over next week or sooner, or whenever you fancy really.

The other extreme is the person who writes you a six-page essay detailing the minutiae of the story leaving you little room to exercise any kind of skill or independent thought. Somewhere in the middle is perfect.

Once you've received your brief, you need to *read it.*

I'm stating the obvious but it's easy to skip over the important details and believe you're on the same page as your editor by osmosis. When you write for a publication or are hired to conduct on-camera interviews, you need to know exactly what your editor or producer is expecting. They are paying you so it's up to you to get what they want.

This is especially true for cover stories, which are just one of the marketing tools publishers use to sell issues or notch up the clicks.

When I returned from Los Angeles to London in 2013, I started writing for *OK!* magazine, whose editorial process back then was unlike anything I'd ever encountered before. It was hugely collaborative and worked quite brilliantly for them at the time. I think that now with all the hubbing, podding, staff changes, and redundancies, things have changed beyond recognition.

Traditionally, *OK!* covers, and by that I mean weddings, baby shoots, baby showers, gender reveals, engagements, are very specific in style and tone, and the editor often had a strong idea of a cover line ahead of the interview.

The cover line is the big statement sentence written in large print on the cover of a publication. It's bold and attention-seeking and draws you in, rather like the child catcher in *Chitty Chitty Bang Bang*. It exists to give you a tantalising glimpse of the interview within should you wish to part with your cold, hard cash. It's essentially a marketing tactic, and a good one can substantially increase sales.

With that in mind, being told what your editor wants will always work to your advantage. Don't be afraid to ask if they don't tell you first. It's always better to know and means you can weave it into the interview.

I've interviewed Tina O'Brien, who plays Sarah Platt in *Coronation Street*, for *OK!* magazine a couple of times now but we go back a long way. Before my trip to Cheshire in 2015 to speak to her, and her partner Adam Crofts, I managed to dig out the first interview I did with her for a weekly TV magazine in 1999. When I showed her the cutting, she fell about laughing.

"I look so young!" she exclaimed.

This particular shoot was to celebrate the first birthday of her son, Beau, and as well as Adam and Beau, her daughter Scarlett from a previous relationship was also in the photographs. It was Tina's first big interview since going back to the *Street* after having her son, and much of our chat focused on that. Tina and Adam weren't married, but we were told they were thinking about it and so we talked about that too.

OK! is known for its magnificent celebrity wedding coverage. Their biggest selling issue (before my time) was Jade Goody's wedding in February 2009. The *Big Brother* and *Celebrity Big Brother* star, who died just a few weeks later from cervical cancer, was paid a reported £700,000 for exclusive coverage of her wedding to Jack Tweed and the issue sold around two million copies.

The heartbreaking cover line for that issue was: "I've had the happiest day of my life, now I'm ready to go to heaven."

In my meeting with the editor ahead of the interview with Tina and her family I was told that an ideal cover line would be something along the lines of "We'd love Beau to be a ring bearer at our wedding" or "Adam is my rock", which addressed the issue of Tina going back to work after having a baby, and also the fact that *Corrie* had just aired a live show, which is all-consuming and nerve-wracking for any actor.

Because I knew what the editor wanted – and also what worked with Tina's personal journey – the end result was a cover line that read: "Tina O'Brien and her partner celebrate their son Beau's first birthday: 'There's no way I could have done the live show without Adam's support – he's my rock.'"

My brief was clear, and I'd been able to plot the arc of the interview step-by-step because I knew where I was going with the story.

Ahead of the interview, I was also upfront with Tina as to the nature of my questions and that helped. Depending on who I'm interviewing and why, I'll sometimes describe before we get into the meat and potatoes of the questions what I'll be asking and in what order. That way, there are no surprises.

Of course, it's not always that clear cut. Time is often tight, the personal relationship isn't in place, or the subject matter makes it difficult. *OK!*'s system worked well because they stuck to a very specific and successful formula. Their interviews are in a lengthy, question-and-answer format and no stone is left unturned.

One thing I was asked to do for *OK!* back then that I've never done elsewhere before or since is share my questions with the magazine's core editorial staff ahead of an interview. I thought it was odd the first time I was asked to email them over to the features desk.

However, I soon came to realise that their system worked brilliantly for them because the team worked on previous stories with the same people, were involved in the contract negotiations, carried a huge wealth of knowledge about all things showbiz, and were very on point with what was happening in the news or other shoots that might cross over. Because of that, their additions were always extremely useful. Never be too proud or starchy to get input from others.

There are also many occasions when you will be well within your rights to question a brief. I did that ahead of an interview for the Australian *Sunday Telegraph* with the actress Drew Barrymore, in Los Angeles.

A commissioning editor had sent me a short brief, part of which was to ask Drew, who was then in her mid-thirties, about the fact that she had puppy fat as a teenager and how she'd gone on to lose the weight.

To me, that seemed totally irrelevant to where she was at that point in her life and also, hugely patronising. I can only think that the brief was pushed out at the end of a long day, it was the first thing that came to mind or they trusted me to look at it and go: "I think not."

This was Drew Barrymore, a uniquely successful screen actor and producer, whose career started at 11 months old when she appeared in a dog food commercial, and skyrocketed to fame after starring in *E.T. the Extra-Terrestrial* at just seven-years-old. She has gone on to star in *Fever Pitch*, *50 First Dates*, *Music and Lyrics*, and *Santa Clarita Diet*.

Her production company, Flower Films, had grossed more than £800 million since opening for business in 1995, mostly thanks to the *Charlie's Angels* reboot, in which she starred and produced. She did all that after a difficult childhood and a teenage decline into drink and drugs, before turning her life around.

No, I was most certainly not going to ask her about her puppy fat.

I replied, politely, to the commissioning editor that I thought a better angle would be looking at Drew's incredible rise from troubled child star to head of a multi-million dollar business and she agreed.

Never be afraid to put your opinion forward. You don't have to be rude but it's always worth asking if you can go in a different direction if you feel strongly that it should.

My intro for the magazine, a Sunday supplement, was this:

Drew Barrymore's latest movie, Going The Distance, *hilariously highlights the pressures of a long-distance relationship but if you think you can write her off as just another fluffy rom-com actress, think again. She's one of the most powerful women in Hollywood, and that's not changing any time soon.*

That was my carefully worded two fingers to puppy fat. Sometimes you have to engage your brain and while I'm well aware this intro won't change the world, it made me feel better to write it. Exercising your judgement and finding the stronger story is always the better option.

Drew in person was petite, polite, and absolutely delightful. She was more than happy to discuss her film production business and why she loves what she does (although she laughed her head off when I called her 'a media mogul').

Times are changing, thank goodness. There was always a sense with actresses before the welcome rise of the #askhermore and #metoo movements, that all that was expected of them was to share their diet and beauty secrets, and what they were wearing. I've been guilty in the past of feeding into this. Sometimes I was desperate to #askhermore but nobody wanted to hear it.

I love the fact that we can go deeper nowadays, and that means you, as the journalist, should always be looking at the bigger picture too. #expectmoreofyourself is my own movement and I'm starting it now.

Meeting Drew was also a bit of a bucket list moment for me because the film *E.T.* has a special place in my heart. I associate it with a precious happy family memory and it always makes me emotional when I think about it.

On the day itself, mid-interview, I decided to tell Drew about this and as I did I teared up, which resulted in her tearing up and us sharing an emotional hug in a suite at the top of the SLS Hotel, in Beverly Hills.

Afterwards I was rattled at my emotional meltdown, and so the next day I emailed her production partner to apologise for ending up a soggy mess in Drew's arms.

I wrote reminding her that I was the last interview of the day and said, The reason I'm emailing is I'm totally and utterly mortified at my emotional response to Drew, who is adorable. I can't remember tearing up in an interview before but the energy in that hotel room was like a warm hug or something. I can't explain it. Something touched me and I was transported back to a very special time in my young life.

Her production partner replied, I just read this email to Drew, we actually loved what you said about E.T. We're big on savoring those rare, happy family moments. Drew and I both grew up in extremely non-traditional, often difficult homes so we know how special and important it is to hold on to those rare happy moments.

That was the only time I ever felt the need to personally connect with an A-lister after an interview and I'm glad that I did (and that it actually got to her). I hope Drew doesn't mind me sharing this personal response but I'm doing it because it illustrates that following your gut and being authentic is okay.

That being said, this kind of malarkey won't always work out as well, but sometimes, when the stars align, it will be the loveliest thing.

The other reason you need to know exactly what is expected of you ahead of an interview is because time is money.

I've been hired by a production company as an on-set interview coach to work with people who may not have had the required media training ahead of an interview with a VIP.

I'm essentially there to instil confidence, advise on lines of questioning, story arcs and ensure that whatever the producers need to hear is said out loud in the interview for that all-important soundbite.

On-set interviews are a different beast to print interviews because you have the huge distraction of a director, producers, crew, lights, microphones, and sometimes the visual whammy of an elaborate sound stage.

I coached two presenters who worked as community managers for a gaming company ahead of the launch of a *Jurassic World* game. The A-lister on set that day was Jeff Goldblum.

Jeff, who played the scientist Ian Malcolm in the first movie *Jurassic Park* was back in the latest instalment in the franchise, and now the voice of the game.

While the presenters were perfectly capable of conducting an interview, they'd never at that point in their careers been in the presence of an A-lister or part of a production as big, and it's an intimidating situation for anyone.

First, meeting someone you're a legitimate fan of (and who doesn't love Jeff?) can take the wind out of your sails. It's also a big movie franchise. Nothing associated with it is small. When I saw the size of the set, even I had to take a breath. It was truly beautiful; all foliage, wooden artefacts, and burning lights. Housed in a huge studio in west London there were five cameras pointing at the three chairs and around 30 crew members busily setting up for the shoot.

I know it was intimidating merely sitting there because I had to pretend to be Jeff ahead of his arrival so that the presenters could get used to their surroundings. I threw them some curveball answers and by all accounts entertained them with my best Jeff, which was less than a pale imitation but did the trick.

Before Mr Goldblum arrived at the studio I sat down with the presenters and reps from the games company and the film studio, plus the director and the director of photography, to talk through the questions and schedule.

My number one concern at the start of the day was: "What do you need from this?" Once we had it figured out, it was then a case of going through the questions, altering them so they were no longer closed ended, repetitive or redundant, and working out where to add in the necessary wording required by the interested parties.

The brief had to be met and as with everything else in production, it had to be done pretty much on the first take as we only had Jeff for a limited amount of time.

Jeff, who is very tall, was charm personified, and if anything talked too much, which is not a problem you have all that often. The brief was met, the required words were said, the questions were answered. The producers were happy, as were the presenters, who ultimately did a marvellous job.

It's not always such a love-in and sometimes you just have to go with the flow, even if you know the end result will probably be a cringe-fest that you will never recover from.

One of my dear journo friends, Melissa Field, who works as a freelance journalist in Sydney, Australia, still has nightmares about meeting Johnny Depp on the set of *Charlie and the Chocolate Factory* and asking him if working on the film had put him off eating chocolate. Ha!

Mel shared this:

I asked him the chocolate question in panic. We were on the set of Charlie and the Chocolate Factory *– 15 international journalists at least and we were on an outdoor* *set when suddenly, Johnny was led towards us. Everyone clamoured around him in a circle, he looked terrified and all the journos started firing questions at him in a virtual babel of accents. It was my first junket like that, and I was panicking that I wouldn't get to ask him anything. I just blurted out the first thing that came to my head: "Has working on the movie put you off eating chocolate?" He'd heard his fair share of dumb/boring questions in the five minutes we'd had with him but the look on his face suggested that mine was the dumbest. THE SHAME.*

To this day Mel still physically cringes at the thought but for the record, no, it didn't put him off eating chocolate.

When I was sent to interview Justin Timberlake and Cameron Diaz, who were promoting their film *Bad Teacher*, I found myself in a similar situation.

Five years earlier the two stars had been, in magazine parlance, 'an item' while Justin was now living with his soon-to-be wife Jessica Biel. I'd been asked by my editor to enquire of Justin: "Was it awkward having movie sex with your ex Cameron?"

It's a really stupid question but they wanted it asked. I would have preferred to have couched it differently. "*Was it difficult working with an ex*?"

So, I asked the clumsy question to Justin, who was sitting next to me. He looked irritated and angrily countered something along the lines of, "*That's a really stupid question.*"

I went bright red. I couldn't argue with him. It was. The conversation moved on, but it was made all the more cringeworthy because it was a roundtable and a group of fellow journos witnessed my shame.

His answer was better than my question, "*We have to believe that there are some people out there who are still friends with their exes. I think our only trepidation in doing this movie was that people would make a big to-do about that. We just really like each other as people and that's never changed even though we've moved on. Our mission is not to do anything but honour that.*"

It was in contrast to a one-to-one interview I'd done earlier with Cameron ahead of the movie *Shrek Forever After*.

She's a giggler and thought the attention their *Bad Teacher* sex scene was getting was funny. She told me, "*Oh sure I did a movie with him, and you don't do a movie with someone and expect not to talk about it. If there was anything, we were touchy or worried about we wouldn't have done it. But we're grown-ups, we enjoy laughing together, and that's what we did on set.*"

This job is often difficult and there will always be uncomfortable moments, but I promise you that the good times will outweigh the bad. Knowing what's expected of you and your copy will help you navigate both scenarios, even if the celebrity you are talking to doesn't understand that.

There will always be a cringe element to celebrity journalism. The entire job is a weird construct and you will often be required to ask a question you think is ridiculous.

But hey, Johnny Depp still eats chocolate so we can all sleep easy at night.

HEADLINES:

Verbal is fine but ask for a written brief too.
Read your brief thoroughly.
Find out what their ideal cover line is.
Don't be afraid to make your own suggestions.
Be nice to good commissioning editors.

CHAPTER THREE

RESEARCH IS YOUR ROCKET FUEL

If you do only one thing before an interview, please let it be some research.

I would also love it if you washed, wore clean clothes, and turned up a little early but first things first.

A well-researched writer will always, repeat, *always* come away with a better story than the one who rolled up at the last minute and is clearly winging it.

A friend of mine who used to work in a government press office told me, "I've had journalists ask me to read things out from the website for them instead of looking it up themselves, which makes me think they must be pretty pathetic journalists and not worth wasting my time on."

She's right. That kind of laziness is inexcusable, and never more so than now because you and around three billion other people carry a library in your pocket thanks to your smartphone. (Source: Statista 2020).

Aged 18 and a cub reporter on the *Southend Evening Echo* it was a different story. Back in those dark ages doing any kind of research was a rigmarole of epic proportions, yet somehow it always worked out.

Everything was trickier, but we didn't know another life, so we just got on with it. This was such a different era I think dinosaurs still roamed the planet (and I'm pretty sure a couple of them worked on the sports desk).

Newsrooms sang to the urgent snip of typewriter keys and intermittently some daft reporter would injure themselves on the spike and have to take themselves off to Accident and Emergency.

What is a spike I hear you cry (and if not, why not?).

Your average HR department would probably faint at the sight of one now, but every journalist had a metal spike on their desk; it was used to physically 'spike' paper copies of stories.

To spike a story means to kill a story. Back in the day, physically spiking your copy meant there was always a record of what you wrote to hand. Useful, but it also meant there was a pointy ten-inch tall weapon of danger sitting inches from your hands.

Throughout most of 1987 – my training period with Westminster Press – I used a trusty, ink-smudged, manual typewriter. Then, horror of horrors, something called "new technology" replaced typewriters and things were never the same again.

Much as I love my laptop, I am sometimes nostalgic for those clickity-clackity days.

The shift in technology was much derided by the editorial department at the time. A few of the reporters on the Echo, including myself, went on strike to fight against the new contracts that came with this digital wizardry. Our band of strikers ultimately negotiated a new deal but after that life on the paper, and on papers everywhere, changed forever.

The newsroom, once a chorus of frantic metal keyboard song, quietened to a dull computerised hum, broken only by the occasional sound of the gnarly hacks on the news desk mumbling through thick cigarette smoke and swearing at nothing in particular.

I'm deliriously happy that I had the chance to work in an old-school newsroom. I absolutely loved the sound of the typewriters, the smell of thc carbon paper, and the thrill of typing a story at a whisker to deadline without making one mistake.

I can still feel my heart racing as I whipped the paper out of the typewriter and ran over to the news editor waving copy around like a mad thing. Every word on that page had to be pristine. There was no option to press delete, scroll backwards, or move paragraphs around in big chunks. You could just about get away with replacing a letter in a word with Tipp-Ex but after that, the news editor would not accept any copy that was splattered with black marks, white blobs, or had lines through words or sentences.

If you handed in a dirty sheet the news editor (always a *he,* in my experience) would throw the paper back at the reporter and growl, "Bring me clean copy!"

Crawling back to your desk, head bowed, you had to start again from the beginning on fresh paper and get it right. No third chances.

Back in these medieval yet rather wonderful times, if you wanted to delve deeper into a story and research it you had to make a request for 'cuts'. These were clippings from old stories that had been logged and filed in the newspaper's library.

From the satellite Southend office, you made a request over the phone to the library situated in the head office in Basildon. You gave the librarian keywords, topics, headings, and dates with a few options around what you were researching so that they could do a wide sweep of their catalogue.

Working in the Basildon office, which was located on a soulless industrial estate, all you had to do was walk down the corridor to the library to speak to whoever was working that day through a hatch, and explain briefly what the story was about.

You then waited two, three or even four days (days!) for them to call you back to say that they'd amassed all the relevant cuttings. After that you'd hustle back down the hallway to collect a manila folder which was hopefully bursting at the seams with musty old clippings of stories relating to whatever it was you were reporting on.

You'd sift through them to see if there was anything of any interest that you could use. It always felt like something out of a Raymond Chandler novel. You'd have to search for clues, dissembling information, poring over the minutiae of every clipping. It was brilliant.

If you were working out of the renegade Southend office, which I did for a couple of years, you didn't even get to see the cuts. You had to call the library and ask them to read them down the phone to you. Your only other resource after that was to chuck a question out to the staff in the newsroom and hope for the best (only for the brave or stupid) or take a trip to the public library to use the microfiche.

I'm actually laughing as I write the word 'microfiche' because it's like I've just teleported myself back to the Neolithic times. A microfiche is a flat piece of film containing micro-photographs of the pages of a newspaper, catalogue, or any other kind of documentation. You slip the negative into the machine and scroll around with a dial to find the right page, and then you either take down notes of the relevant information or print it out.

And oh look, there's a stegosaurus!

Sadly, newspaper libraries are now also a dying breed, and many have already been consigned to history. Another former Westminster Press trainee recalled recently going back to her local paper in Buckinghamshire to look up something in their cuttings library for a book she was writing.

As the reporter from the paper showed her around, she asked about the 'splash' that day (the main news story on the front page) which was about the council closing a local hospital. She told the reporter she'd worked on the original story back in the day and mentioned that all the background would be in the cuttings library and wondered aloud if they'd think of running a 'then and now' feature. She suggested they interview the people who had saved it back then about what they thought of the new threat.

Despite the fact that this was a great idea and exactly the kind of reporting that should be done on a local paper the reporter she talked to was totally uninterested in doing any further research.

He told her that they never went into the library and that – hold the front page! – they were getting rid of it. Not digitalising it but just chucking it out.

It's so sad. We can't afford to let our history disappear and on a local level it's worse as these are the stories that knit together the fabric of a community. I simply can't fathom what was going on in that reporter's head that he didn't leap at the chance to tell a better story.

A few years after my modest beginnings on *The Echo* I was hired as the Letters Editor, then Production Editor and writer on the teen magazine *BIG!*. This was the early to mid-nineties, and Take That, East 17, and the casts of *Home And Away* and *Neighbours* were our cover stars. We didn't have a library at Emap, so we used a cuttings service called Tasiemka.

Described more recently as 'human Google', Tasiemka was an agency run by a woman called Edda Tasiemka, who had escaped Nazi Germany, and with her husband Hans, started collecting newspaper and magazine cuttings.

This already sounds made up, but it isn't.

Their home in Golders Green was filled to the rafters with stacks of newsprint and magazines, and after Hans died in 1979, Edda registered the company and became the saviour of research-hungry journalists everywhere.

At the time I was using the service, I thought I was calling some high-powered office block with a staff of thousands, not some random woman's living room in a suburb of North London.

My friend Joanne Hawkins, who I worked with on *BIG!*, and who is now a journalist based in Australia, remembers it going something like this: "I have very fond memories of Tasiemka at *BIG!*. I remember you used to call them and a woman who sounded a lot older than me answered the phone by saying 'Tasiemmmmka' in a long, drawn-out fashion. You gave her the name of the celebrity you wanted some cuts on and then waited a couple of hours, if you were lucky, for the fax machine to start spewing out your newspaper clippings."

If you were even luckier, you would be couriered a manila envelope, but you always had to send the cuttings back. If you didn't send them back on time someone would call and tell you off!

It seems archaic now, but it worked perfectly well for us back then.

But while the manner in which we do our research has changed, the reason we do it stays the same; it's good for business.

Celebrities by their very nature like attention. They want to feel loved and cherished and admired, and what better way to do this than by learning all there is to know about them? By showing that you care.

Look, you may not care but here it behooves you to pretend to care.

The opposite of caring is not knowing anything, getting it all wrong, and pissing them off. And that is not good for business, or for your writing.

At the April 2010 LA junket for the movie *Predators* I interviewed actor Adrien Brody for the cover of *The Scotsman's* weekend magazine.

I'd been told by various journalists that Adrien was 'difficult' but before I go on, I'll say that I've been told this about many actors ahead of my interviews. Most of the time I found my fellow journalists' assessments to be wrong and this was no exception. Adrien was most personable.

I clearly recall the interview at the Hotel Casa Del Mar in Santa Monica because a) it's a beautiful ocean-front hotel in one of my favourite parts of town, and b) I'd worn a new pair of the shoes I'd bought especially for the junket.

Big mistake.

Mine was the last interview of the day and because the shoes didn't fit properly, by the time I walked into the suite for my one-to-one interview with Mr Brody my feet were killing me to the point of distraction. I was sort of *Misery* hobble-shuffling. Not the strongest start.

I knew I couldn't concentrate while I was in pain and so in an interview first for me, just after our introduction, I asked him if I could take my shoes off. He laughed and said, "Of course". Then he added, "I think I'll do the same," which is why we both found ourselves curled up on opposite ends of the sofa, me barefoot and him in his socks. Cue lovely relaxed chat.

This was a marked difference from his roundtable earlier in the day.

One of the journalists, who hadn't bothered to check how old the actor was beforehand, asked a question that I'm paraphrasing but wasn't a million miles from, "What's it like to have just turned 40?"

This irked Adrien because he was only 37 – and in actor years being 40 means 106 – and you could see it got to him.

Getting something so basic so wrong is unacceptable. Even if you hadn't had the time to do any other research for whatever reason you could at least ask the junket publicist or look up the man's bio on the way into the room on your phone. IMDb and Wikipedia, while not always correct, are your friends here.

Adrien laughed it off but the atmosphere in the room changed and not for the better. Later, when another journalist asked a question along the lines of "What have you learnt recently?" he replied dryly, "That I'm younger than I look."

It was a blunder that had grated and there was a strong sense that he'd put up a wall. That is exactly what you don't want to happen in a celebrity interview.

You are already fighting the elements of time constraints, over-anxious publicists, the actor's desire for privacy and general interview jitters, so why make things harder for yourself by ballsing up a basic question?

At the end of that same day while we were talking privately, he referenced it again but not in a way that impacted my interview badly. I'd got off to a good-humoured start because of my ill-fitting shoes (thank you wide feet!) and our conversation flowed.

As I recall, we ate biscuits and drank herbal tea. It was a good experience and I'm grateful he didn't hold the age mistake against me for merely being in the room with someone who was so ill-prepared.

Getting someone's age so wrong seems minor but if your one job that day is to interview someone and you don't know the most basic of facts about them, what are you even doing there?

Another illustration of how research is your friend came when I was commissioned by the Saturday magazine for *The Express* newspaper, to interview the original Captain Kirk, William Shatner, who had just published his autobiography, *Up Till Now.*

He was doing a small amount of press specifically for the book but he was also busy shooting the ABC network show *Boston Legal* (playing the egotistical Denny Crane), which was in its final year.

Because of his schedule, he only had time to meet me at his place of work which was fine by me, but the glitch was that the showrunners had banned journalists from the set.

Mr Shatner's publicist told me that I was to arrive at the Raleigh Manhattan Beach Studio gates where my name would be on the guest list. I was to tell anyone who asked that I was ‘a friend of Bill’s’, who was there simply to shoot the breeze with their old pal who was filming.

I rather love a silly situation so was totally game for this minor subterfuge and launched myself into it whole heartedly. For all intents and purposes, I was ‘a friend of Bill’s’ and you should know that I’m a loyal friend so that was that.

But the reason I bring up this interview is to say that before I even knew I was going to be cast that day as ‘a friend of Bill’s’, I did my due diligence and read the book from cover to cover.

I underlined passages that interested me and that I thought would lead to interesting conversation or that I could challenge him on. I wanted to find something that would connect me with him on a personal level and that would give me more of an insight into the man. An authentic connection is the sweet spot.

I was particularly drawn to the passages in the book about his early life in Canada, where he was born, where he talked about the battles he’d had with his father, who wanted the teenager to join him in the garment industry. Young Bill wasn’t having any of it having set his heart on a career in the arts.

My grandpa Nat was a tailor in the East End of London, and I could see parallels between his life and that of Bill's dad. Because of my family history I had some understanding of how immigrant families worked hard to improve their life for the next generation.

After the 'friend of Bill' situation was explained to me the fact that I'd read the book proved doubly invaluable; I now had plenty of insider information to draw upon if anyone was to challenge my spurious friend status.

What ensued was a rather comedic day of me being first introduced to Bill in his dressing room. He was dressed in all white and lifting weights.

Before I could start the interview proper, he was called to set, and I watched him film a courtroom scene with the magnetic James Spader.

Bill did his bit and then James had to recite a ridiculously long monologue. It took a few takes and the scene was reset a few times. In those moments, after the director yelled, "Cut!" Bill would motion to me (a sort of imperceptible nod) and then I, his close personal friend, would follow him back to his dressing room. This happened many times throughout the day and goodness only knows what everyone was thinking. Actually, I can probably guess exactly what everyone was thinking but it was most definitely not that.

We'd get back to his dressing room, start the interview again and a few minutes later there would be another knock at the door and I'd then have to follow him back to set, where I was once more seated behind the director to watch the action.

Also on set that day were some friends of the director (actual friends) and they asked me what I was doing there. I told them I was 'a friend of Bill's' and then getting a little too deep into character, I regaled them with tales of my visits to Bill's ranch, horse riding with him and his then wife Elizabeth, and enjoying big family barbecues, teasing them that I knew what went into his secret barbecue sauce.

"That's awesome," I remember the lady saying to me before launching into yet another question about Bill's horses. I fumbled for a bit and thankfully the director yelled cut.

The scene was reset, Bill nodded in my direction, and we headed back to his dressing room with me thanking my lucky stars I didn't have to come up with a ridiculous story about tacking or hacking or something.

Because of the stop-start nature of the interview, I knew it would be hard to find some kind of continuity. What saved me in this situation was my research.

I won him over when I asked about him and his dad, and the garment industry. He actually stopped what he was doing, looked at me and said, "You've really done your research."

Something shifted after that. Our discombobulated interview became more cohesive. Bill knew that he was talking to someone who had taken the time to learn his story and do the work. He may even have been flattered. Whatever the psychology, I got a better interview because of it and he opened up in a way that he wouldn't have done before.

I love this passage from my transcript where Bill talks about growing up as the child of Eastern Europeans in Montreal. He said, "Acting came out of nowhere. There was some disappointment that I wasn't going to follow my father in the schmutter [Jewish slang for clothing] business. My father was a salesman, he started his own firm and was struggling, he made suits – not something that a rich man would take but it wasn't the $5 suit either. He had aspirations to do better, but he was doing as much as he could and then along comes a son and two daughters, and the son goes to university and he struggles to pay for all that. The reward, now as a father, would have been send him to college; he comes back with an education, he's assimilated and he's going to propel us to grand heights. My father was not possessive or jealous or ambitious but when I didn't fulfill that it was a great disappointment. I think far more disappointing than he let on. Nothing else interested me and the thing that least interested me was the clothing business. I'd go there and he'd tell me here's how we do this and we'd go on a sales trip for the day, to an outlying town and I found myself tired. I'd go in on a Saturday morning and lie down on the tables after school was over. He'd take me into the office, work for a half day, I'd be with my father, I'd lie down on his cutting tables and fall asleep. I had this ennui, I became lethargic. Whereas when I was working on plays and musicals at college, 18-hour days were nothing."

It was a lovely story, and one that gave a huge insight into his early struggles.

So I finished my day at the studio as maybe not quite a true friend of Bill but enough of a new connection to have found a way to make the story sing.

Before then and to this day, I spend a long time delving deep to dig up an angle or any nugget of interest that might give me the edge in an interview.

Think of research as one of the most important tools in your toolkit. It is as important to you as a phaser is to the crew of the Enterprise. And the reason I know that is because I am 'a friend of Bill's'.

Just don't ask me for the barbecue sauce recipe because as I said I'm a very loyal friend and my lips are sealed.

HEADLINES:

Research is your most important tool.
Find a detail that speaks to you.
Use that information to make a connection.
Thorough research means a better story.
Feel free to take off your shoes.

CHAPTER FOUR

MAKING A DYNAMIC FIRST IMPRESSION

There are around 90 crucial seconds from the time you walk into the room to the interview starting. Those precious 90 seconds, where you're introduced to the celebrity and settle down to start your interview, will massively influence what happens next.

Why?

Because that's your opportunity to make a dynamic first impression.

There's a quote that has stuck with me over the years and I pass it on often because I truly believe in the philosophy. Dr Jill Bolte Taylor said, "Take responsibility for the energy you bring into this space." Dr Taylor was a Harvard scientist who suffered a stroke and while unable to speak as she lay in her hospital bed she noticed how the energy of the doctors and nurses, translated into touch or tone of voice, gave her comfort. So much so that she had the quote above posted onto her door.

Many times I heard journalists grumble about how miserable or difficult their famous interviewee was and yet I've rarely experienced anything truly awful. I wonder if sometimes it's because they didn't *bring it* on the day. Even if I had to do star jumps in the corridor to get my energy levels up (this happened many times), I always made sure I walked into a room giving off a positive energy.

The energy you bring with you into that 90 second space in time is *currency*. It's a vital part of your toolbox and should be exploited to the max. Don't be a grey cloud.

While you're not a performing seal, you are there to use all your skills to elicit a good interview and sometimes, like in many things we do in life, you have to stick on a smile and breeze along as if nothing bad is happening.

Junkets in particular are pressure cookers, so it pays to keep a sunny disposition.

You should also look professional. I'm no fashion expert, as anyone who knows me will attest, but dressing smart, clean, and you-appropriate should also figure into your first impression timeline.

While I was based in Los Angeles, my brilliant stylist friend Henny Letailleur always made sure I looked the part by lending me key pieces. Kris Jenner loved a rather smart Tom Ford handbag, while an AllSaints dress that had a dash of gothic milkmaid going on and a turquoise Marc Jacobs creation were repeat successes.

I soon learnt that people with money notice. So, if like me you can't be trusted to dress yourself, make friends with someone talented who can.

Once you've checked in to the junket, the publicist will tell you the approximate time your interview is happening, and then you will sit on whatever chair happens to be available in the suite they've booked, chatting to/or ignoring your fellow journos, drinking coffee, and sampling all the lovely patisserie.

During this time, you should probably go over your questions. Junket interviews are always tightly scheduled which means that as soon as you cross the threshold from hallway to inner sanctum, you're on the clock. It pays to know what your opening question is and have a good idea of how the interview should flow so that you can get everything you need. More on that later.

Publicists working on junkets are generally overworked and trying to fit too many journalists into too small a time frame. It's junket Jenga. Nerves are jangly and if we're being honest, everyone (including the talent) just wants to go home and binge-watch Netflix. But you need to rise above all the stress and focus on your first 90 seconds.

I can clearly remember waiting outside Courteney Cox's penthouse suite at The Mondrian in Beverly Hills, ahead of an interview I was doing with her for the cover of a Sunday supplement.

She was promoting *Scream 4* and as I waited I tried to focus on the job ahead instead of thinking about the fact that I was about to meet Monica from *Friends*.

We'd negotiated a full 30 minutes of interview time and all was going well until the publicist leaned in close as we were waiting for the journalist before me to wrap up and leave, and said, "Just to let you know that you can't talk about David Arquette (her then husband, they were having marital problems) and you now only have ten minutes for the interview. Is that okay?"

My heart stopped. "No, not really. I can't make a cover story happen in ten minutes," I replied.

Also, the editor wanted a relationship line, so this episode was becoming the one that was turning into a big, fat nightmare.

The door swung open and the publicist urgently whispered as we walked in together, "Please, just do this ten minutes for me and we'll sort something out afterwards."

Me, panic rising, "Okay, but we need to figure it out quickly."

Inside I was spinning but was now firmly in the 90-second zone, the clock was running, and so I put all that aside and blasted forward towards Courteney all handshakes (pre-COVID obviously) and wide smiles.

Gear change, happy voice. "Hello, Courteney, so good to meet you!"

We sat down to chat and after what seemed like two minutes, during which time Courteney brought up her relationship without any prompting, the same publicist stepped in and said, "Last question."

I must have looked utterly pained because Courteney said, "Do you have enough for your story?"

"No, it's for a cover for our *Sunday Magazine*. I need at least 20 minutes more to make this work and even that's cutting it fine."

Courteney immediately suggested that I speak to her manager, who at the mention of her name, appeared to fall out of a cupboard on the other side of the room.

Fun junket fact: *It's rarely you and an A-lister alone in a room together. It can happen but there's generally a publicist or assistant present (usually wearing all black and angrily bashing away on a laptop), and quite possibly another six people who could be entourage, family, friends, or executive types, hiding in the adjoining bedroom or bathroom. These are the ones that tend to leap out at unexpected moments.*

Out of the corner of my eye I saw Courteney's manager, who had been listening, fall out of a cupboard but realistically was more likely a door to the adjoining suite. She said, "Would it be okay if we arranged for Courteney to call you Saturday afternoon?"

I did some cover story maths. It was midweek and I was filing the copy that Sunday for publication the following week. I had to trust that Courteney Cox would call me. As I was leaving the room, I gave her manager my contact details and hoped against hope that Monica from *Friends* would not let me down.

At 2 p.m. that Saturday, Courteney called on time as planned from her home office. We clipped though the rest of the interview and I got everything I needed.

She even apologised for making me work on a weekend. What a class act.

The point is this, you have to be prepared at any moment to deal with any number of obstacles but you only get one introduction and you don't want to stuff it up. Establishing a positive energy is key.

You should be doing this everywhere work related. I always made of point of getting to know the names of valets at the various Beverly Hills hotels because I was doing almost exclusively movie junkets and I was usually at the Four Seasons two or three times a month. It made life a lot easier to pull up in my beaten-up Ford Taurus or later my clunky PT Cruiser, park alongside the Mercs, Porsches, and Lamborghinis and breezily announce, “Me again!” The disparity in riches was never lost on me or the valets. We’d always have a little banter, I tipped well, and never had to wait too long for my car at the end of the day.

So how do you approach the celebrity in those 90 seconds?

Well, I’ve always found it useful to smile, look them square in the eye, say an enthusiastic hello and – if it’s your thing or even appropriate in this era of coronavirus – offer a handshake. Eye contact is vital throughout the interview and not just the first 90 seconds but it’s essential you make that connection immediately.

It’s the smile that really works, though. Not one through gritted teeth or wildly manic (you don’t want to come off as nervous), but a genuine, happy smile that is also reflected in your eyes.

You don't have to tell me how cheesy that sounds. It's a veritable bubbling fondue of Swiss cheese with extra cheese doing the can-can on the side next to a melting raclette and a choir of Babybels. Believe me, I can be as grumpy as the next person but a natural smile and a genuine, "How are you?" will always start things off on the best foot.

And why wouldn't you be happy to be there?

You have to look at the bigger picture which is: you're meeting quite possibly the hottest/biggest/sexiest/most feted celebrity on the planet. You are sitting with them in an intimate space, and you should feel privileged to be there. One day you might even write a book about it.

And even if we're not talking A-listers – the levels of celebrity are vast and complex – you still need to bring that good energy with you.

Even so, first impressions don't always go to plan. I was dispatched to interview the incomparable Betty White, who was promoting *The Lorax* in 2012.

Sometimes you get the dream job and Betty ticked all my boxes. She's a legend and a funny lady having starred in *The Mary Tyler Moore Show*, *The Golden Girls,* and more recently *Hot in Cleveland*, as well as *The Proposal* with Sandra Bullock and Ryan Reynolds (the other Ryan). She's bona fide Hollywood royalty and I was enthralled to be in her company.

I've found that the older the interviewee, the better the interview. Older A-listers in particular are relaxed, they've seen it all, and have the best stories.

Betty was 90 years old when I met her and exuding a gorgeous vitality and lightness of spirit. Her first impression energy was genuinely the warmest I've ever bathed in and thankfully on that day, she had enough for both of us.

The interview, a cover, was due to take place in her spacious trailer on the Universal Studio lot but it's all a bit foggy. I'd flown back from London the previous day and was horribly jet-lagged. I remember they had giant candy fountains in the media tent so I overdosed on E-numbers, which was probably the worst thing I could have done. I remember saying hello to her co-star Danny DeVito, who was a delight, making it his business to stop and chat to all the press in the tent.

By the time I was escorted to Betty's trailer later that afternoon I was deep breathing, star-jumping, and trying to energise my flagging body in any way I could but every synapse was shutting down. The dreaded lag was mounting a hostile takeover of my body and mind, and I could barely put one leg in front of the other.

As I walked up the tiny stairs into Betty's trailer I managed to trip myself up, falling straight through the open door ending up flat on my face, while simultaneously propelling my open bag through the air and scattering the contents onto the carpeted floor.

As Betty looked on in horror, I pulled myself up onto my feet, clumsily scooped up my stuff, walked into the nearest table bruising my thigh and crying out in pain before crumpling next to her on the L-shaped sofa.

"Are you all right?" she asked with genuine concern.

At this point I was on the verge of tears so I merely nodded as I fumbled for my tape recorder, which I then promptly dropped knocking over a glass of water.

Aside from setting myself on fire I'm not sure what else I could have done to have made a bad situation worse.

There was a beat.

"Would you like a cocktail?" she asked.

What a legend.

I didn't accept the cocktail but a cup of coffee and cookies, which appeared on a china plate out of nowhere.

That was absolutely not the first impression I'd hoped to make on Betty White but after I'd stopped doing my bull-in-a-china-shop schtick I explained to her that I was jet-lagged and we settled down to an interesting conversation.

I loved hearing about her early days in Hollywood and how much she was enjoying her latter-day career opportunities.

I asked her (pertinently) how she stayed so nimble and energetic. She told me she ate a hot dog (no mustard) and fries every day for lunch and enjoyed a cocktail every night at dinner.

Here's her recipe in her own words, "Always Grey Goose vodka on the rocks with a big wedge of lemon. Squeeze all the juice out of the lemon and throw it in the glass."

Maybe I should have accepted her offer of a stiff drink after all?

During our conversation Betty also said this to me, "If you hear me complain about anything you should throw me away."

A Hollywood legend she might be but she was also grateful to be in the room. We can all learn a lot from Betty.

Good energy can also win you friends, particularly when it comes to publicists.

Scarlett Johansson was doing press for the film *We Bought A Zoo* in New York.

I'd been flown out there for another cover story, which happened maybe half a dozen times during my time in Los Angeles. What a gift those jobs were. A free flight to New York, a luxury hotel room in Manhattan for a couple of nights, a per diem of $125 that just about covered the cost of a hotel breakfast, and the rare chance to catch-up with New York-based friends. Usually I'd take a stroll around Central Park as the junket hotels were always nearby, but this was memorably the fifth rainiest day in the Park's record and it was torrential outside.

The press day took place at the Ritz-Carlton New York, Central Park and I got there a little earlier than usual so that I could dry off and also watch some of the footage of the film, which was based on a true story about a widowed British writer who had bought a failing zoo in Devon.

Nine times out of ten you'd be expected to attend a screening of a movie in advance of an interview but on occasion, if the movie was still being edited, you'd be shown clips, trailers, or a rough cut.

I have a bad back as a result of scoliosis and subsequent back surgery, so I'm often in a constant low-level state of discomfort, however the flight from LAX to JFK had triggered shooting pains through my lower back and legs.

I'd taken a couple of ibuprofen but on the morning of the chat the pain was getting out of hand so someone in the press pack gave me a super strength painkiller. I'll be honest it looked like a horse tranquillizer and while I'm not usually in the market for that kind of thing, I was desperate to numb the excruciating pain somehow.

This confession is the backstory (excuse the rotten pun) to what happened next. And while this is not exactly Hunter S Thompson's *Fear and Loathing in Las Vegas* levels of drug use it was a lot for me. I like a whisky cocktail or two, but drugs have never been my thing. I don't even like to take antibiotics.

I realised as I was waiting for my interview with Scarlett that I was entering another dimension. The world was getting a little fuzzy around the corners.

As I was sinking into my comfortable junket armchair gazing out from the 12th floor over a rain-sodden park, the publicist asked if she could have a quiet word with me.

HOW DID SHE KNOW?

WAS I DRIBBLING?

No, it wasn't that.

I'm paraphrasing here but the conversation went something like this: "I'm sending you in next. The first two journalists have upset Scarlett by being rude and asking stupid questions and I know I can trust you not to do that. She told me that if that happens again, she's going home. And I really think she will. But she can't go home. She has to stay. I need you go in there and do a really great interview. Please don't upset her."

Okay, so this was a proper situation. I stood up tall and put my best non-drowsy, non-horse tranquillizer face on and told her that I could be trusted to do absolutely that.

I also realised at the same time that I was started to lose feeling in my hands.

The publicist walked me along the corridor to Scarlett's room, and said, "Good luck," and then nudged me through the door.

Surprisingly, Scarlett was all by herself and seated rather formally at the room's circular dining table.

"How are you?" I said and smiled as widely as I could. We shook hands and I sat down opposite her. I set my Dictaphone to record, calmly placed my questions in front of me, and was silently cheering myself on at this show of total and utter professionalism, when at about the 90 seconds mark the horse tranquillizer hit another level and I exclaimed, "*We Bought A Zoo*? WHO BUYS A BLOODY ZOO?"

Then I started laughing and no matter what I did, I couldn't stop.

Thankfully, Scarlett also started to giggle. "You lot bought a zoo. He was a Brit!"

And then we both fell about laughing.

This wasn't good energy; this was ridiculous energy but somehow it was working.

About ten minutes into the chat she looked me in the eye and said, "Are you buzzed?"

I paused for a few seconds before coming to the speedy conclusion that honesty was the best policy. I told her, "Yeeeees…but there's a really good reason."

Then I explained about my back problems, the flight, and the horse tranquillizer.

She thought it was hilarious and offered me some of her trail mix.

The rest of the interview was a succession of giggles and nonsense. Because it was an interview for a fashion mag, I had to ask her what she was wearing. She had a belt on with an 'H' clasp. Anyone worth their fashion salt knows that's the sign of a Hermès belt but not this space cadet.

Scarlett said the word 'Ermez' about three times before I exclaimed, "Oh, HERMS!"

I'm sorry, Hermès, I will never say your name wrong again. Your belt is lovely, but I had no idea it was pronounced 'Ermez' before Scarlett gave me a lesson in fashion French. She thought that was hilarious too.

After the interview, we hugged goodbye. That's not usual either.

The publicist found me in the media room a few minutes later and said slightly bewildered, "I have no idea what you did in there but she's in a completely different mood. She's even laughing. Thank you so much."

"You're welcome," I said, as I floated away down the hallway on a fluffy cloud.

Now, just in case legal have a problem with this story, I'm not suggesting for one single second that anyone should down a mysterious giant blue pill before an interview but on this occasion it did the trick as my back pain disappeared for a few precious hours. But do not try this at home, kids.

Another astoundingly ridiculous yet successful first impression I made came when I met Hugh Jackman in 2011.

I was completely overexcited to meet him as I'm a musical theatre fan and he started out treading the boards. Have you seen his Tony Awards performances? Go look.

I remember zipping along Sunset Boulevard the morning of the interview playing the soundtrack to the musical *Sunset Boulevard* at full blast, singing along out loud, and generally getting ridiculously overexcited at the thought of meeting Wolverine.

The junket was for the movie *Real Steel*, and was at the Four Seasons Beverly Hills, and as it turned out, I was the first interview of the day.

My brief was to get an in-depth chat with him about fatherhood for *Sunday Magazine's* Father's Day cover story.

I'd been allotted a good 45 minutes, which I was very grateful for because the two children he shares with his wife, Deborra-Lee Furness, are adopted, and they are advocates. So aside from the usual topics, I wanted to make sure we honoured that side of things too.

I was the first journalist to arrive by 8 a.m., which was early. My interview had been scheduled for 9 a.m. but they'd asked me to turn up in advance just in case Hugh was ready to get cracking ahead of schedule.

So I bounded in (wearing the gorgeous turquoise Marc Jacobs dress that Henny had lent me), and was told that he was already ensconced in a suite down the hallway and did I mind going in now?

No, I did not mind.

A young publicist led me down the hallway and as we walked, I started to hear the song 'Sunset Boulevard' in my head again to the point, when I walked into the room I started SINGING IT OUT LOUD.

As I stepped towards Hugh, I raised my arms and blasted in his general direction…

"Sure I came out here to make my name
Wanted my pool, my dose of fame
Wanted my parking space at Warner's
But after a year, a one room hell
A Murphy bed, a rancid smell
Wallpaper peeling at the corners."

(All credit here to the songwriters Don Black and Christopher Hampton.)

After I'd sung the last line with a sort of insane flourish, I fake collapsed onto a sofa.

Hugh stood there laughing and said something I will never forget, and that speaks to his generous nature and sublime acting skills. "That was great. You've got a good voice."

The publicist looked horrified. She went to sit down in the corner of the room and said to Hugh, "I'll be right here."

To which Hugh replied, “No, no, you can leave us alone. I think I’ll be able to handle this one.”

She reluctantly backed out of the room and I said to Hugh, “I’m so sorry, I’ve never sung myself into a room before but I couldn’t stop myself.” And then we had a little chat about his musical theatre roots which was just great.

As the chat progressed, he was funny, open, and engaged. The energy in that room that day was Broadway level excellent. I half expected to be handed a Playbill on the way out.

After Ryan Gosling, I get asked about meeting Hugh Jackman all the time (with an uptick in interest after he released *The Greatest Showman* in 2017). We talked for a good 45 minutes and the interview was by far one of the best I’ve ever done with a star of his calibre. If you find the photograph I asked to be taken post-interview, you can see that I’m the happiest woman on the planet.

And while those first 90 seconds were as unconventional as having claws shoot out of your hands, I think it was the fact that I was clearly full of excitement that made it all the more special.

Hugh was generous enough to humour my singing, Betty my jetlag, and Scarlett my back pain. But above all, and with every other interview, most of which were far less dramatic, the energy I tried to bring with me was always good, always positive, and always well-intentioned.

HEADLINES:

The first 90 seconds count.
Bring good, dynamic energy into the room.
Smile and ensure you have eye contact.
Be the journalist they can rely on.
Don't be afraid to be yourself.

CHAPTER FIVE

THE DEVIL IS IN THE DETAIL

You are now in the room.

Sitting opposite you is a very famous person.

It's time to get down to business and keep the machine moving.

Funnily enough, even after all these years, I still get nervous. But that's okay. Nerves are good. They keep you sharp and they keep you focused.

Not every interview will be in a room or a five-star suite at a hotel or on a movie junket.

I've interviewed celebrities in photographic studios, the back of cars, vans, and buses, catering trucks, in bars, pubs, restaurants, kitchens, castles, nightclubs, warehouses, art galleries, shopping centres, TV studios, radio stations, at parties, backstage, front of stage, under a stage, dressing rooms, green rooms, bathrooms, location houses, their own houses, on beaches, in the middle of the desert, a shipping port, a Florida swamp, and once on a ranch in Montana.

Not every interview will require you to write an intro or set the scene, but for those that do you need to have your wits about you.

Setting the scene by way of the introduction is a device that enables you to bring the reader into the room with you. It infuses the piece you're writing with exquisite colour and its own unique identity.

This, I think, is the delicious antipasti of the story and the place to show your writing skills and hopefully a little personality. To do this, you need to soak up as much detail around you so that the reader can imagine themselves there with you.

One thing that's easy to forget doing this job is that many people don't get to meet famous people in real life. You are their eyes and ears.

They don't know what celebrities look like up close or the way they drink, eat, or what they smell like, the shape of their hands or how they sit on a chair. But you do.

Will they pour you a drink, or order one?

Play with their hands or their hair?

Sit cross-legged or pace the room?

Recite poetry?

Pace the room?

Smoke?

Or just stare oddly into the middle distance?

These are the details that will set your story apart from everyone else's. You have limited time to soak up this colour so from the get-go you need to set yourself to 'sponge mode' and soak it all up.

Journalist Adrian Deevoy, who I don't know personally and have never met but whose work I've followed since his days on *Smash Hits*, did a one-to-one interview with Madonna for *Q magazine* in June 1991.

It set the scene so brilliantly that I remember it all these years later, and so I tracked it down online. Here's part of his opener where he finally meets Madonna in her home in Los Angeles:

Displaying the self-conscious grace of a small girl attempting to keep her mother's shoes on, she moves slowly and deliberately across the bare floor to the window. Her hair is blonde and, like her music, has black roots. It is scraped back from her face into a small ponytail. She is wearing a loose, green, lattice-work top – a string vest on drugs – with small glass beads at each intersection. It does not unduly tax your powers of X-Ray vision to see that she is also sporting a black brassiere. Beneath this combination, it is alarmingly obvious, lurk the celebrated Ciccone bosoms.

The sort of trousers favoured by fashionable toreadors complete the ensemble. As a concession to comfort she has on her feet a pair of old green espadrilles, fraying slightly around the toes. She looks sickeningly healthy and radiates fitness. She is smaller than you'd expect, even when you were expecting her to be small. She is, in the flesh, uncommonly beautiful.

This is the Jackson Pollock of storytelling colour.

At that time Madonna was the international call sign for not just independent women but overt sexuality (which believe it or not back then was still shocking to the larger demographic), and he did a sublime job of presenting the physical embodiment of that to the reader.

The rest of the story is an equally brilliant masterclass in setting the scene. Do yourself a favour, find it online and read the whole interview. I truth or dare you.

When I first moved to Los Angeles my friend Mark Tungate, who was also on my NCTJ course at Westminster Press, and who is now an esteemed author and writer living in Paris, said this to me, "Enjoy the first year. That's when you notice everything, when it's fresh and exciting."

This is also a good rule of thumb for working a celebrity junket interview and for setting the scene.

Notice everything. Enjoy it. Keep it fresh and exciting.

I was commissioned to write my first A-list profile shortly after arriving in Hollywood in 2007.

It was with Cate Blanchett at the Beverly Wilshire, and I remember it well because I wasn't at that point MPAA (Motion Picture Association of America) accredited. This accreditation is how publicists ensure they're not letting any old lunatic into a room with the talent (just accredited lunatics).

I had to jump through many hoops to prove I was legit which included sending them many examples of my previous work. I was also required to show references from my current editors and previous editors before they'd allow me to meet with Ms Blanchett.

After I'd done all that for the first interview, the rest fell into place and I soon had enough cuttings and bylines to become fully accredited.

I might have been green around the edges but I was prepared and almost certainly channelling Mr Deevoy with this intro:

Sweeping into a plush suite on the eighth floor of the Beverly Wilshire hotel, with its impressive views over the Hollywood Hills and the famous white-washed sign, Cate Blanchett looks like a modern-day Katharine Hepburn, a role she played to great effect in Martin Scorsese's The Aviator.

Dressed in fashionably baggy grey tweed trousers, dark-green silk shirt, and black ballet pumps, she oozes old-school charm. However, after a firm but enthusiastic handshake, the 38-year-old clearly has other things on her mind.

"Could you hold on a moment? I have to pee," she says, before dashing off to take in the marble splendour of the en suite, leaving me and a press officer to make small talk.

Minutes later, she's back. "Is there any way we can get into the minibar?" she asks no one in particular, tugging at the handle of the tiny fridge. Unfortunately, it's locked but, not one to be put off from a late-afternoon snack, she finds a packet of macadamias and rips off the foil cap.

"Care for a nut?" she offers, sitting down on the sofa. I decline, worried that I might end up choking in front of an Oscar winner, and it's only then that she sits back, lets out a huge sigh of relief and props her feet up on the coffee table.

It's impossible not to notice Blanchett's incredible bone structure. How pale her skin is; how delicate the lines around her eyes are. She's thoughtful and quiet and comes across as someone who could answer all life's mysteries – a sort of female Dumbledore. Her voice is soft and hypnotic. If I weren't here to work, I'd probably curl up in a ball at her feet and start purring.

After this interview my editor asked me if I thought Cate was pregnant as she'd heard rumours. I said no, I didn't think she was.

Read my intro again.

Snacks. Toilet break. Feet on coffee table.

Of course she was pregnant. I didn't ask her and I'm loathe to guess at any pregnancy because it's a biggie if you get it wrong but more to the point, it's none of my business. Or yours. Many celebrities choose quite rightly to keep their pregnancy under wraps until they're good and ready.

However, after that massive oversight I found myself looking for signs of pregnancy in all A-listers (this was a short phase as you shall discover), and a few weeks after interviewing Cate I became convinced that Jennifer Garner was with child when I met her at the Four Seasons ahead of the release of *The Kingdom*.

She hugged a giant pillow to her stomach the whole time. That was my evidence. It wasn't much m'lud but it was all I had.

I told my editor I thought she might be pregnant but didn't include it in the copy because that would have been complete and utter speculation as I hadn't asked her outright (and why would I?).

Jennifer, who it has to be said is a very nice lady, gave birth to her son Samuel approximately two years later so unless she's an elephant, my bump spotting skills are severely lacking. I've never bothered to predict a pregnancy since because it's just wrong and as I said above, none of my business.

Sometimes you're gifted an intro without having to do anything. And the thing to remember here is that with junket interviews everything is so samey that the smallest detail can be magnified to intro status.

I met Kate Beckinsale one-to-one for another Sunday mag cover, for *Underworld: Awakening*, again at the Four Seasons, and throughout our interview she was fiddling with her belt. Not much I know but it gave me an 'in'.

At the time I remember being irritated by that stupid designer belt because it was distracting her from my questions.

When I suggested she take it off, she firmly said, "I won't let it beat me."

This belt was becoming the third person in our relationship and a serious opponent.

Her waist was tiny. I don't think I could have got that belt around my thigh. But that belt was a tad tinier. However, she persevered and because we'd noted it in our conversation, the belt formed part of my intro.

My intro:

Kate Beckinsale is having a wardrobe malfunction. Her wide Ghadah Paris belt, the perfect complement to the gorgeous black Gucci dress she's wearing, keeps popping open. Reed thin but with just the right amount of tabloid-friendly curves, she's determined that this testing nod to fashion won't get the better of her. "I just won't breathe out", she laughs, as she adjusts it again, and sits up straight. "This belt is fashionable but evidently not functional!"

I think the anecdote gives a good insight into her personality (and mine as I clearly have an aversion to designer belts).

You don't get to the top in Hollywood without determination and steel, and she has both. Both are beautifully demonstrated by belt-gate.

Another tip you need to follow, mostly because I say so (#kidding #notreally), is that even though everything is recorded these days, and only a handful of journos use shorthand, in my humble opinion you should always take a notebook and pen into the room.

Most journalists now solely rely on recording devices, but I think pen and paper make up an essential part of your toolkit.

Why? Well first, it's a nice prop. It's comforting holding a pen and I think it gives off an air of, if not quite authority, then preparation.

When it's you versus the celeb, you need to use everything available to feel as if you're on a level footing, so try the pen and paper trick.

Second, it gives you the chance to scribble down, "eats peanuts, toilet break, feet on table, soft voice" etc. without interrupting the flow of conversation.

You're not going to be able to say keywords out loud for the recording so you have to be able to write them down. These are the unique details that set your story apart and so mid-conversation, and without seeming distracted, you must be simultaneously noting anything that makes your story more interesting.

I've trawled through my transcripts and here are some snippets of my notes that I used for colour...

Adrien Brody: Kicks off shoes, snuggle on sofa, jeans, and military style shirt. Olive skin, gorgeous green eyes. (I think I was slightly taken with Mr Brody.)

Jane Lynch: In car, on way to record a song for a *Rocky Horror* episode.

Cameron Diaz: Gets up, closes door to block out noise.

Emily Blunt: Brunette hair, caramel highlights. Huge diamond ring. Nibbling on crudités.

Hugh Jackman: Phone vibrates. "I'll ignore."

Mila Kunis: Wearing all black with impossibly high heels, hair swept back and up.

Josh Brolin: Packet of yellow American Spirit cigarettes on table.

Fun fact: *After my interview with Josh Brolin I picked up his cigarettes instead of my Dictaphone which I shoved in my bag. I only noticed my mistake halfway down the hallway as I like to check immediately that the interview had been recorded.*

I had to run back to the suite to find him waiting, with a big 90-second smile on his face, holding my tape recorder in his hand.

"I suppose you'll want this back?"

"Fair swap," I said handing him the ciggies.

Stuffing your intro with personal touches will set the piece apart. Also, there's no point being at the celebrity's home, baby shower, or wedding, or indeed in touching distance of a star, if you're not going to include all the dazzling detail. The reader ultimately wants to be taken on that journey with you.

The eagle-eyed among you will notice that I interviewed Jane Lynch while she was in her car. The piece read differently. Sometimes you need to engage in some fancy wordplay to make it sound like you're in the room with the celebrity when in fact they're on the phone [see Chapter 15, The Challenge of the Phoner].

It's not perfect but there are times when geography and schedules get in the way of a cosy sit-down chat.

When that happens, I usually open the conversation by asking three key questions:

1. Where are you?
2. What are you doing?

3. Have you been doing anything today I should know about?

If you're lucky, you might get a nice anecdote about baking cupcakes with the kids, going for a dress fitting or horse-riding lesson. All of this colour is great for an intro, particularly if it's a profile piece. If nothing is forthcoming, you have to fudge it a bit.

My intro with Reese Witherspoon, which was done on the phone, opens:

Reese Witherspoon boasts a smile that could light up Sunset Boulevard – and she's been using it a lot lately. Her latest movie, Water for Elephants, *based on the best-selling novel by Sara Gruen, is about to hit the big screen, and her personal life has been filling column inches thanks to lavish wedding number two.*

It sounds like I was in the room with her, right?

And here's my opener with Kristin Davis, who I talked to on the phone about her work for Oxfam:

Kristin Davis is talking at high speed. She's in the middle of a complex story about one of her fact-finding trips to

Mozambique, to demonstrate how Oxfam has empowered women in impoverished, far-flung communities.

Her speech pattern was so quick, it was definitely worth a mention and also it made her sound passionate about her charity work.

Colour is a little more difficult for on-camera work – especially when you do the production line junket interviews that last about three minutes – but you can still notice what the celebrity is drinking and ask what it is. They may have a cold, they may be on a weird health kick, or wearing a T-shirt with a political slogan and this might be useful to include in the final edit (but at the same time it might not make the cut, or in the case of the T-shirt be blurred out for rights reasons).

You may also want to bring along a prop to mention, or a gift.

Search YouTube for a clip of *This Morning* presenter Alison Hammond's chat with Harrison Ford and Ryan Gosling for *Blade Runner 2049*. She ends up drinking whisky with the actors which makes for an absolutely hilarious interview. And yes, she got to interview Ryan Gosling and she didn't even have to leave London to do it!

Your biggest gift is a quirk of behaviour that's more than just a celebrity sitting opposite you. You can use anything that jumps out at you, although sometimes, you may choose not to.

I remember waiting to interview January Jones, the actress who played Betty Draper in *Mad Men*, and being deposited into the hotel suite before she arrived. The heating was at 80 plus degrees (that's 26 degrees in new money) so I flicked on the air conditioning as it was far too hot in the room for me.

Ten minutes later her assistant walked in, and much to my dismay the first thing she did was switch the a/c off and turn the heating back on.

January eventually appeared, said hi, then lay down on the chaise longue and covered herself in a blanket. I sat at the end of it feeling much like the therapist Betty was simultaneously seeing in the show.

I didn't talk about it in my piece probably because I was short on space but if I'd had had more room, I may have mentioned it.

Rather brilliantly Matthew McConaughey, who I interviewed for *The Lincoln Lawyer* in 2011, spent the entire interview pacing the room.

That was a fun job as it was the only three-to-one interview I've been asked to do, which meant it was me, Matthew and two other journalists (from different territories). I've never been in an interview where the celebrity wouldn't stop moving.

I wrote for the Australian *Sunday Telegraph*:

Matthew McConaughey struts into the suite at the Four Seasons Hotel in Beverly Hills looking suitably rugged and as if he was born to wear the snappy Dolce & Gabbana suit that drips off his broad shoulders like a lazy Sunday morning. He takes a slug of water, then insists on pacing the room during the interview. McConaughey's new movie, The Lincoln Lawyer, is a triumphant return to form after years in rom-com land, and you can tell he knows he's back in the game.

Again, the colour in the story gives you a beautiful insight into the man's character and energy.

Shia LaBeouf, on the other hand, led me out onto the balcony of the hotel so that he could smoke throughout our chat. He was 21 and the hottest young actor in Hollywood (for about five minutes concurrently with Ryan).

For the cover of *Sunday Magazine*, I wrote:

Here in LA, there's an air of excitement surrounding the highly anticipated Indiana Jones and the Kingdom of the Crystal Skull. And it's not just because this is Steven Spielberg's first Indy film in 20 years. No, this buzz is all about hot new Hollywood in the shape of a 21-year-old actor whose name confuses the most intelligent reader, Shia LaBeouf. (Let's get that small detail out of the way: Shia rhymes with 'Hiya' and LaBeouf is pronounced 'Le-Buff'.)

So when he eventually bounds into the hotel where we've arranged to meet, it's something of an anticlimax to find that he's, well, just a 21-year-old guy, who's desperate for a smoke. He immediately asks that we move all conversation to the patio, so he can puff.

"Yes, I smoke," he admits shamefacedly. "It's probably the worst thing I do. I leave wet towels on the floor, too. I don't think I'm the quintessential guy to look up to right now because I'm still building myself."

Sweet. Troubled. Honest.

One thing I consistently did after all these junket interviews was to make more notes.

I could always be seen mumbling to myself as I walked down the hallway back to the press room, usually into my tape recorder. Not just because I was mad but because I was eager to capture everything.

I'd note any further standout detail so that I would have it to refer to later.

Celebrity interviews whizz by in a flash. You think in the moment that you'll remember every little detail afterwards, but you won't.

In the moment, it's all so clear and visceral. Weeee! Your adrenalin is pumping and here you are, in a small space with a very famous person.

You think it'll be easy to remember what they were wearing, drinking or doing but chances are you'll draw a blank later on because of all the other distractions and detail crammed into your head. So, mumble away if necessary.

I also love it when the celebrity eats. You don't often get a chance to talk over food but when you do, it's perfect.

As I mentioned earlier in the book, I interviewed *Mad Men* star Christina Hendricks for *Grazia UK* just as she was exploding onto the global stage, during the show's first season.

We met at the legendary Chateau Marmont on Sunset Boulevard, which is just the most evocative location for any interview.

Her unique selling point as herself, and also as her TV character Joan Holloway, the advertising agency's all-knowing secretary turned shareholder, is that she is a curvaceous, confident woman.

My intro was this:

The patio restaurant of LA's Chateau Marmont is packed with entertainment's elite, talking shop over towering plates of Sunday brunch.

This being Hollywood, however, none of the women appears to be actually eating anything. Then Christina Hendricks appears at the stop of the stairs, the famous hourglass figure accentuated by a nude silk dress. In a sea of skinny, Christina is a positive breath of fresh air. She exudes class, glamour, and the old-school sexuality of Marilyn Monroe, Jayne Mansfield, and Sophia Loren.

'Sorry I'm late, I hope we've still got time to get everything done,' she says oblivious to the fact that every man in the room still has his eyes on her. "Can we order some food?"

We order lunch; Christina opts for chilled tomato soup with a round of cucumber and avocado sandwiches, wash down by a latte. "I used to say that I had opposite anorexia," she tells me. "Every time I'd take my clothes off, I'd look in the mirror and think: 'I feel like a woman and I like myself this way'."

What I love about this colour is, like Kate Beckinsale, it gives you a glimpse of the real Christina Hendricks. This is a woman who will eat a substantial lunch before a photo shoot. What's not to love?

Ironically, what I also remember about this interview is that after we'd eaten, we went upstairs so that she could go into hair and make-up ahead of the shoot. For some reason all Christina's clothes provided that day were the wrong size. All smaller. Awkward.

Disaster was averted thanks to Christina's patience and the stylists' quick thinking. She isn't the boring Hollywood ideal; she's got a beautiful figure that many women admire and can identify with.

Hopefully, we're now entering an age where women don't have to be so stick thin and cookie cutter (and also where it doesn't always have to be the focus of any interview as it has been in the past. Believe me I've noticed it a lot in my own writing as I've been editing this book).

Cookie cutter is what you don't want in your writing. Absorbing detail and colour and being able to set the scene is one of the ways in which you can avoid making everything and everyone sound the same.

So don't be afraid to allow yourself to soak it all up, don't be afraid to use a pen or be that person talking into a recorder in public.

This is the job, embrace it.

HEADLINES:

Take a pen and notebook into an interview.
Look to add colour to your story.
Absorb everything around you.
Set yourself to sponge mode and soak it up.
Remember, little details show personality.
Write down more detail as soon as you leave the room.

CHAPTER SIX

THE POWER OF A KILLER QUESTION

One killer question can change your fortunes.

The right one can unlock a front-page story, birth a sizzling cover line or worldwide exclusive you had no idea was lurking all along.

It's a delicious moment when the response to your question turns out to be pull-quote gold (the pull quote is the large type, stand-alone quote you see on the page).

Any journalist who is after a good story, and particularly those who are interviewing celebrities under pressure or against the clock, knows what a massive relief it is to get anything that solidifies your interview, or finds new ground with a fresh angle or line.

Before I get into the meat and potatoes of how to plan your line of questioning and think about the flow of the interview, I want to share with you a couple of anecdotes about how just one cracking question can turn an interview on its head.

This one question doesn't have to be clever. Sometimes it can be downright pedestrian but for whatever reason you have somehow chosen to utter the right words in the right order at the right time. Sometimes it can be as simple as: "Is there anything else you want to tell me?" Other times it doesn't even have to be that complicated.

Remember Donny Osmond from the start of the book?

Well, here's my Donny story.

When I was a toddler Donny Osmond was the biggest pop star on the planet.

He and his sister, Marie, and their brothers, The Osmonds (later including Little Jimmy) dominated the charts with their bubblegum pop. Donny and Marie sang duets together while looking pristine, healthy, and exceptionally toothy.

Young girls would lose their minds when cherubic Donny, whose biggest hit was 'Puppy Love', sang his feathery songs wearing his flashy, pastel-coloured seventies' suits with their fashionable wide lapels and flared trousers.

Collectively, the Osmond family have sold over 100 million records. They were so big throughout the early seventies, the media even had a name for the hype, and that rather uninspiring name was 'Osmondmania'.

I wouldn't class myself as an Osmond fan. Despite my talk of manual typewriters and Tipp-Ex, even I was too young to be a fan of anything at that time except *Play School* and naps.

My teen crushes didn't kick in until Duran Duran and Spandau Ballet were on the scene in the early eighties but as a kid, I clearly remember the Osmonds as a benign and shiny television presence.

Then, a long time after the heady days of Osmondmania, I found myself being sent to a small independent record store in Southend-on-Sea to cover a personal appearance by Donny Osmond.

Donny Osmond in the late eighties was by all accounts living in a sort of celebrity no-man's-land. These were his wilderness years, although the album he released in 1989 had produced a synth-pop hit called 'Soldier of Love' and was seen as a comeback. In subsequent interviews he has revealed that during that time he was on the verge of bankruptcy and also suffering from depression.

He was most certainly down when *The Echo* came knocking but not quite out for the count. He would eventually launch a fabulous comeback which culminated in him and his sister booking a long-standing Las Vegas residency in 2008, and Donny winning *Dancing with the Stars* in 2009 (partnered with Kym Johnson).

But rewind a few decades to my first stab at a celebrity interview.

While I was mildly excited, I was also distinctly unimpressed. I was 20 and to be frank, I couldn't care less about Donny Osmond. I was too young to appreciate his superstardom and I was certainly too young to understand how he was struggling to find his place in the world as time and trends moved on.

Thinking back, I was clearly looking a fantastic story smack in the face, but I didn't see it. To me, he was washed up.

It actually hurts me to write this now having gained more empathy through living an actual life but I want to be honest, and so here's a fun fact: *Donny Osmond is only ten years older than me. At that time in my life, however, he seemed positively ancient.*

But I was also young and eager to prove myself, and so when I was given the assignment by my news editor I knew I had to do a good job. I just didn't really have a clue what that might be.

I was informed that the news desk wanted to splash a photo of Donny on the front page of the paper's evening edition but aside from that I wasn't really briefed as to content. It was my job somehow to rustle up a few captivating words to go with the picture.

It was a 'roll up with a photographer, throw a couple of questions in Donny's direction, and write an extended caption that would make a strong front-page filler' kind of assignment.

This was long before the days of Google, so I couldn't easily access Donny's entire life history or discography on my phone, and I didn't have enough time for a library search. I asked around the newsroom what people thought of him, got a handful of standard filthy replies and that was that.

What *was* I going to ask him?

What could I expect to get out of him in such a momentary meeting?

The record shop had been told to expect hordes of fans eager to meet their idol. This intrigued me. I had visions of the police holding back screaming women as they desperately tried to crash through the barriers.

But I still really didn't have a clue what to ask.

Before I left the office, I asked my straight-talking news editor Colin Newman what he wanted from the piece.

He could tell I was struggling to get a handle on the story. He was excellent at his job and as a newbie to the

Southend news desk I felt compelled to prove I was worth his time. We were a tight-knit bunch in that rebellious satellite office, in daily competition with the bigger newsroom based in Basildon. Reporters would open the paper and search for their own bylines while mildly cursing at others who had landed the meatier stories. This (mostly) friendly rivalry and enthusiasm kept the stories coming.

I'd proved I could hold my own, though. Small tangent. On my first lone nightshift, which was called 'drag', I scooped not one but two front-page stories. The splash carried my first front-page byline and happened to be the long-awaited news that the cancer unit at Southend Hospital had been saved. It was a big campaign that had been rumbling on for years and I just so happened to be the person covering the desk that night when our local MP called to say the happy announcement was imminent.

My first call after that was to Colin, who guided me through my what-to-do-next checklist, which involved getting reaction quotes from other high-profile campaigners. I remember my heart thumping as I typed up the story in a joyful reportery whirl. The next afternoon, I walked into the office to the claps, cheers and yes, jocular jeers of my co-workers, waving copies of the paper in my direction and yelling at me to stop getting splashes on drag as it made them look bad. (For those who are interested, the second front-page story that day was about a dog with an injured leg.)

I think Colin had faith in me throughout my time as a news reporter. I know I'm not the only one in that office who wanted to do a good job for him. He was tough but fair in equal measure.

As I left to meet Donny, he said, "Get him to tell us that he's excited to be here and that he's looking forward to seeing Southend Pier."

I wrote his words down verbatim on my notepad.

Southend Pier is the longest pleasure pier in the world coming in at a whopping 1.34 miles. It's the town's major landmark, and while I was working on *The Echo,* it always seemed to be closed for business because it had either been set on fire or smashed in half by errant tankers.

It's open now though, and you should visit if you can. TV chef Jamie Oliver films *Jamie & Jimmy's Friday Night Feast* in a fake café at the end of it.

The Echo's photographer and I arrived at the record store. There were no crowds. No barriers. No police. It was eerily quiet.

Inside the shop a random punter and two women, who were in their early thirties and wearing Donny Osmond merchandise, were excitedly waiting for their idol to appear.

There were three members of staff milling about, plus me and the photographer. So less than ten people were waiting for Donny.

I dutifully took down the names and ages of the two super fans and got a couple of quotes along the theme of how excited they were and how little sleep they'd had due to said excitement.

Suddenly, the man himself and a couple of other guys appeared through a doorway at the back of the store and the ladies squealed. He greeted them warmly and our photographer snapped away. After a minute or so there was an awkward lull, so I stepped forward to say hello.

I remember thinking that Donny wasn't quite present in the moment. He was on tour so it's quite possible he'd lost track. Or perhaps he didn't care? He seemed melancholy (as I said, he talked about his depression around that time many years later).

I asked him about his new music, and he gave me a short quote and after that I was floundering. This was all new to me. How could I fill the space?

It was an awkward situation and I could see that 'his people' were getting ready to whisk him away.

I looked down at my notebook and saw it.

The question.

I raised my voice and said, “So Donny, are you excited to be in Southend and looking forward to seeing Southend’s famous Pier?”

“Yeah, I am, yeah, very excited.”

And then he was gone. I’m pretty sure he didn’t know he was in Southend and I’m fairly certainly he’d never heard of our famous Pier but I had my quote and the paper had their headline.

These slim pickings will sometimes be your reality.

You won’t always be served everything you need from an interview on a plate, but one question can make it all right.

All kudos to my news editor who told me to ask something that seems so simple and intuitive to me now but as a trainee news reporter was completely out of my reach.

Side note: *When I told my friend, Julie Seddon, this story during the writing of this book she laughed. Julie, who was a news reporter and also my mentor on the Evening Echo, revealed that Colin had told her the same thing was she was sent to interview the late broadcaster and author Bernard Levin. (Colin, you’re busted!) However, her interview threw up the interesting detail that Bernard actually used to visit Southend Pier with his nanny. (All hail Colin, you are a genius!)*

That evening, there was a lovely photo of Donny smiling on the front page of the paper with a headline that told our readers how happy the 'Young Love' singer was to be in our town and that he was looking forward to seeing the Pier.

And that was that. That was my first celebrity interview. Donny got a meaty mention for his album and I got a story on the front page of the paper. Win-win.

Another time one single question gave me a home run was during the mid-nineties when I covered a press conference for the TV show *ER*.

I think it was in its second season so by this time, George Clooney, who played handsome Dr Doug Ross, was the hottest male on the planet and interest in the show was intense.

I was working as the deputy showbiz editor on a now defunct TV listings magazine and was told by the editor as I left for the press conference to get a story for the cover.

Stomach lurch.

I'll be talking about press conferences later in the book but it's hard to get an exclusive when you're in a room with a hundred other journalists and they're all listening intently, or at least have turned their recorders on.

A handful of the cast were in attendance. Julianna Margulies, who played Dr Ross's love interest Carol Hathaway and went on to have even greater success on the TV show *The Good Wife*, and Anthony Edwards, who played Dr Mark Greene, were both on the panel. I sat through the press conference and didn't have the chance to ask a question which meant I didn't have my cover story.

As the 'talent', as those with talent are known, were leaving the room I sidled up to Anthony Edwards and thinking on my feet said to him as quickly but as quietly as I could, "Have you ever needed to use the ER?"

As he was hustled out of the room with me in hot pursuit, tape recorder held aloft, he told me a short story about having to go to the emergency room recently because one of his children had been taken ill.

It was no more than three lines and took under 30 seconds to tell but as he walked away I shouted after him, "Have you told anyone else this story?"

"No," he said and smiled. I smiled back. I had my exclusive. Dr Greene, you will always be my favourite TV doctor.

One question. The right question. One cover story. Job done.

But how do you find this elusive journalistic pearl?

Striving to find something different isn't easy. It's important that you stay current, soak up the world around you and keep on top of industry news.

Use your research and also your imagination. You should ask something that will evoke an interesting answer or that moves the story forward. This could be a follow-up to a previous story, a reaction to something in the news or just the act of digging around your subject for any hidden gems.

Most importantly, use your own judgement. What vibrates your journalistic antenna?

As you get more experienced, your instinct will tell you if an answer to a question will make a strong cover line. Sometimes the line is so good it will also make national and sometimes international headlines.

I've interviewed the Australian model Miranda Kerr a couple of times. The first was in 2010 before she'd given birth to her first child Flynn, who she shares with ex-husband Orlando Bloom.

I was invited onto a closed set to observe a shoot for the David Jones Summer 2010 campaign, and observe I did. I was barely able to stand at 5 a.m. and drank a barrel load of coffee, while Miranda positively glowed as she writhed in front of the cameras, snacked on fruit, and sent a barrage of emails on her BlackBerry.

By the time we talked over the phone a few days later it had been announced that she and Orlando were engaged. We had a little chat about that and also easy breezy topics such as her visits to see her grandmother in Australia and the importance of getting enough sleep. My bed is "the biggest luxury in my life", she told me.

It was acceptable content that gave the reader a glimpse into her private life but certainly not front-page stuff.

I filed the copy but before the interview hit the stands, it was announced that she and Orlando had married in secret and that they were expecting a baby.

It's safe to say that in this instance I pretty much missed the big story. I was denied a top-up interview and had to rewrite the intro to include the updates.

Happily, a few months later Miranda gave me another shot at grilling her and the answer to one question in particular made front-page news across Australia and the rest of the world.

After Flynn was born Miranda went back to work fairly quickly, and when *Sunday Magazine* organised a shoot with her in Palm Springs, she requested me, which I'll be honest, is always very flattering.

I asked her if she'd used pain control during labour and she told me that she'd decided against any form of it. I was intrigued and asked her if it was worth it and to describe the experience.

Here's an excerpt from the interview from July 2011 which includes her answer in full:

Flynn's arrival into the world wasn't easy. Miranda's labour lasted 27 hours and apart from being induced, she didn't so much as sniff a drug. The pain was intense – Flynn weighed almost 10lbs at birth – but the model says she found the experience empowering.

"I've never been through so much pain, but I was totally present the whole time, focusing on my breath and meditating. It was good to be able to go through that and have Orlando there with me by my side. I couldn't have done it without him. Just to have his support was a really wonderful experience," she reveals. "I was thinking the whole time – how do women do this? And if other women have done this, then I can do it too. I was determined. I actually thought I was going to die at one point and left my body. I felt like I was looking down on myself. I could see myself lying there – the pain was so intense. And then he came out, and we finally met each other, and it was the best

thing ever. I think once you go through something like that nothing else fazes you – it puts everything into perspective."

As I listened to her answer, I knew it would cause ripples.

Sunday Magazine's cover line was: 'Miranda: I Thought I Was Going to Die.' The strap line underneath read: 'Model mum Miranda Kerr reveals the truth about her drug-free birth.'

I wasn't surprised that the magazine had pulled out that one line. Whenever any celebrity has a near-death story, it's always newsworthy. What I didn't realise is that the answer to that one question would make the front page of the main Sunday paper and subsequently picked up around the world.

I had no idea it had caused such a stir until a friend in Sydney emailed me a snapshot of the Sunday paper that showed my story taking up most of the front page.

It's always nice for a profile to get a lot of love but that headline came from one question. And sometimes that's all it takes.

Other times you need to look at your story as a whole and particularly when there's a time crunch, you need to have an idea in advance of how your story is going to move forward. You can only do that if you've prepared your questions properly. And that, my crazy horses, is what we're looking at in the next chapter.

HEADLINES:

One question can change your fortunes.
Think on your feet as the moment is fleeting.
Dig around for nuggets of information that can be translated into a killer question.
Use your instincts. What do you want to know?
Even a short answer to a good question can be cover material.

CHAPTER SEVEN

WHEN TO MAKE YOUR MOVE

How and when you ask a question is as important as the question you ask.

Sometimes a situation requires you to be, how I shall say it, a little flexible.

More than two decades on I'm still processing the time my friend Kirstin Chaplin, who was then features editor of pop weekly *Smash Hits*, was flown to Florida to interview Aaron Carter, the younger brother of Backstreet Boy Nick Carter.

He was only nine years old when his first album was released, eventually going on to sell a million copies. In my opinion no minor should be doing press calls or speaking to the media in the manner of an adult.

The interviews were held at a hotel but Aaron, quite understandably, wouldn't come out of his bedroom suite. He was physically *underneath* his bed playing with his toys, so

Kirstin had to get down on the floor just to say a friendly hello.

Aaron wanted her to join in his game. She didn't but instead asked him her questions in that sing-song voice you use when speaking to small children. I remember her being quite shaken by the entire encounter, as any sane grown-up would be.

That's an extreme example of anything you might have to do but who knows, the world is a strange place.

During junkets actors who are underage are always accompanied by a guardian. Chloë Grace Moretz, who was only 14 years old when I interviewed her for the movie *Hugo*, was accompanied by her mum, brother, and their dog Jackson (a very good boy and most excellent guardian).

If I've ever had to interview the child of a celebrity, I'll always run the questions by their parent or parents first.

I always ask the parent if I can use the funny or cute thing that a kid might have said or done while they were running around when the shoot was being set up, having their photo taken, or during lunch, etc. It makes for nice colour, especially for an intro when you're setting the scene. But I would never use the words of a child without permission from a grown up.

I don't like to ambush people. That's not my way. Never has been and never will.

But I've seen other journalists use snark, snip, and sarcasm to force their way through an interview.

I remember rescuing the late, great actress June Whitfield, who played Edina's mum in *Absolutely Fabulous*, from a tabloid journalist at a TV junket in London. The journalist in question was aggressive, leaning in close, and giving June, at that point in her ninth decade, no room to manoeuvre.

I put a stop to that by gently leading June to a nearby seat so she could have a breather. I felt the journalist's intense stare from across the room, but I didn't care about that. Even if your editor is demanding an exclusive, you're on deadline, and the world is on fire, you've still got to be mindful of the people you're talking to.

Another time at a junket in LA I was at a roundtable with Jamie Foxx. I think one of the newspaper journalists in the room clearly had an agenda, and that was to make Jamie Foxx look unintelligent.

I don't know why that would be anyone's agenda, but I've seen it happen more than once. This approach always irritates me because you don't get the best out of anyone by putting them on the defensive. You'll get a reaction but that's it. But you know, even amoebas react (urgently googles 'amoebas reacting' to make sure this is true. Yes, it is true, continue…), but a human can give you so much more if you treat them well.

Jamie Foxx is a brilliant entertainer. He is a comedian, a musician, a Grammy winner, and he also won a Best Actor Oscar for his portrayal of Ray Charles in the 2004 film *Ray*.

This journalist was using unusually long and obscure words. Words that would be your best friend in Scrabble or *Countdown* but not necessary at a movie junket.

The journalist pushed and pushed and pushed until Jamie looked so uncomfortable, eventually saying, "I don't know what that means…"

Yoiks.

I jumped in. "I think what they mean is this…" And put what I thought they were saying into simpler words.

He was clearly grateful.

I happened to be the person asking the next question as we went around the table in order. I went in next tactically with a question relating to his early career as a stand-up comedian in order to put him back squarely into his comfort zone. He looked relieved, answered fully and hilariously. For the rest of the roundtable he answered all the questions asked by the assembled journalists but only looked at me.

I'm sure that irritated the hell out of everyone else but they got the answers to their questions, and all was ultimately well.

I didn't speak to the Scrabble champ seated to my right after the roundtable – and I'm not here to put my job or any journalist down in any way – but why shame someone because they're not as educated as you? The journalist in question was trying to get a rise out of him for a headline. That's not my style. It's up to you I suppose if you want it to be yours.

Jamie Foxx was just one of the people I saw around the table that day. I wasn't there to interview him or file copy based on that chat. But I did feel compelled to step in when I thought things were getting weird with the line of questioning.

A week or so later I was in traffic on the 101 freeway in Los Angeles as is often the way. If you ever spend time in LA be sure to make peace with driving, your car, and the traffic. Always ensure you have plenty of water, coffee, and snacks with you. In the boot/trunk keep your beach towels, chairs, and cool boxes as well as your snowshoes, skis, and winter coats for the mountains, and an earthquake kit. You need to be prepared for anything.

Sitting in barely moving traffic I looked across the lane to my right and saw that the man in the car next to me was none other than Jamie Foxx.

He looked over, recognised me, smiled, said “Hi”, and then started doing that ‘call me’ thing people do with their hands. It made me laugh. I nodded and mimed I’d call him back. Then the traffic moved, and he drove away with one last wave.

Nice one, Jamie. I consider that my thank you.

(Not that I’m looking for thank yous but just as an aside, please thank me every time I do something nice for you or we are no longer friends).

Obviously, you will have to sum up every situation and then follow your instincts.

I remember eons ago getting a cover story out of a five-minute phone call with the actor Neil Morrissey, who was in rehearsals for the sitcom *Men Behaving Badly*.

I was working for the aforementioned TV listings magazine and was briefed to phone him at the studios and that I’d have 20 minutes. Just before the call I was informed that our chat had been reduced to five minutes, which was something to do with him having a cab waiting.

Five minutes? What can you do in five minutes?

Quite a bit it turns out, as long as you approach it with the right attitude and a lot of energy.

The feature was a moral dilemma quiz: What would you do in this situation? Choose a, b, or c, and say why, sort of thing, so thankfully it was a bit of fun and nothing heavyweight.

He took the phone call while still in the rehearsal studios on a landline, and I, taking a punt he'd have a sense of humour, said immediately, "Right, listen up, Neil, I have some multiple-choice questions for you to answer, we have just five minutes and we're going to talk really fast. Are you up for it?"

He was. "Go!"

Five minutes later, after a lot of fast talking, silly banter, and laughing, I had the page in the bag, and he jumped into his cab.

Not everything is funny.

One of the most painful experiences in my life happened when I was a trainee journalist. I'd yet to even join the *Echo* because Westminster Press, who then owned the paper, sent their trainees to St Leonards-on-Sea to undertake six months journalism training as part of the NCTJ Proficiency Test. Like now, you had to pass shorthand and typing, local government, central government, and media law exams. Without them you couldn't work as a reporter.

I was very young; 18 to be precise and not particularly worldly. I'd lost my grandpa when I was little but that was it. Death hadn't really touched my life at that point in any significant way. I've always been empathetic, but I most certainly did not have the wherewithal to process emotions in the way that I do now.

On the night of the 6th March 1987, while I was living in St Leonards, the MS Herald of Free Enterprise capsized just after leaving the Belgian port of Zeebrugge, killing 193 passengers and crew. Many of them were British.

The ship was headed for Dover when it left the harbour with its bow-door open. The sea immediately flooded the decks and within a few short minutes the ship was lying on its side in shallow water.

It was a terrible tragedy and front-page news for months after the event.

Once a week, during our training we were sent out to cover our local beat; this was a patch of the town that we covered as our own and used to source stories. As one of the youngest my beat was nearest to the journalism centre and as I recall, I spent a lot of time hanging out at a second-hand clothing store called The Glimmer Twins. The people who ran it were lovely laid back, hippy-goth types and as this was winter, anywhere out of the cold was a blessing. They always made tea and fed me biscuits.

I also used to call into the local pubs and chat to the landlord and staff. One of them was called The Cask and on this particular day, one of the staff asked me to talk to a regular customer who had lost three family members in the recent ferry disaster.

"When?"

"Now, they're sitting over there."

Oh.

As I write this now, I can feel my blood run cold again as it did that day because I knew I was about to encounter something I wasn't ready for.

The pub was launching a fundraiser called Cask Aid and a family member wanted to talk about their loss.

Before I knew what was happening I found myself sitting in front of a grieving man who I remember softly asking, "What do you want to tell me?"

After that it's a blur. I know I had my notebook out and made notes in shorthand but that's it. I was spinning internally.

I wasn't used to handling people's raw emotions. I certainly wasn't used to this level of unabashed grief. There were tears from everyone including myself. It was excruciatingly difficult for me to ask questions about and listen to the answers.

I wrote down the words 'Cascade' in my notes.

That's one thing I've never forgotten.

The fundraiser was called *Cask Aid* and I wrote it down as *Cascade*.

Since then I've never failed to spell check the name of anything.

After a couple of hours, I zombie-walked back to the training centre. I saw my teacher Peter Unsworth, who was a hard as nails Yorkshireman (who had covered the Moors Murders court case), and who immediately saw something was wrong. He told me to go home, not write anything, and come back the next morning where we'd discuss it with the group.

I did exactly as he said. The next day I wrote up the story about 'Cascade' and gave it to Peter. The local paper, the *Hastings & St Leonards Observer*, actually ran a factually correct version of the story in one of their later editions.

Thirty years on I still think about that cold, rainy day in St Leonards. It has stayed with me every step of the way and I can still feel the grief. It's a hugely important touchstone for me because in that moment aged 18, I grew up. I saw that I'd been gifted the chance to see the responsibility this job entrusts you with.

Those people were waiting for me to come into the pub so they could tell me their story.

Even now I look back at that in disbelief. Really? I must have looked no older than 12. But I was a journalist. I was the person they were relying on to get their story out there. It was a steep learning curve.

After that, my first in-depth report for the *Evening Echo* was a series following the lives of people who attended Alcoholics Anonymous, Al-Anon, and Ala-teen. I went to all the meetings, tracked real-life stories, and translated the emotion I saw in those meetings into words on the page. I'm still proud of that report.

Fun fact: *the series was so good it was nicked in its entirety by a now long-defunct weekly women's magazine (and I wasn't able to get any money out of them no matter how hard I tried).*

But I couldn't have done that story without 'Cascade'.

I'm telling you this now because celebrity led or not, what we do is real. It can be serious, moving, and emotional.

"What do you want to tell me?" can open up the door to so many worlds and one that isn't always glitter, giggles, and showbiz.

We are in a very privileged position.

Journalists have this incredible licence to walk into the lives of complete strangers and ask them questions.

There aren't many other professions that allow you to do that and not be locked up or laughed at.

Sometimes, we get asked to walk into the lives of strangers who happen to be famous and ask them some things too.

You never know what the winning question will be that brings that wall tumbling down, and if you do have an inkling, then you'd better know how to ask it.

How do you talk to Hugh Jackman about adoption?

How do you get Dame Julie Andrews to talk about losing her singing voice?

How do you ask Justin Timberlake and Cameron Diaz about having fake movie sex after their real-life relationship ended?

These are all questions I've asked of famous people in my time. The latter, as I wrote earlier, was not well received by JT.

You can't just go blundering in and hope for the best. Well, I suppose you can but why would you want to do that if your endgame is to get the best story and not just any story?

'Read the room' is a phrase that works well here, especially when it comes to celebrity. Moods change and your line of questioning has to reflect that. You have to be aware of when may or may not be the right time to follow a particular line of questioning.

I've noticed over the years, particularly at junkets where press day seems to dovetail with a huge news story about the talent's private life, that you need to test the room temperature. Not literally but in terms of mood.

I've interviewed Charlize Theron four times; three of them were one-to-one interviews and the other was a press conference.

We always got on well but the last time we met, which was in 2012 ahead of the release of her movie *Prometheus*, there was something afoot. I sensed it as soon as I walked into her suite at The London West Hollywood hotel. She seemed more guarded than before. Despite the fact we'd established something you could call a friendly rapport over the course of our previous interviews (not a real friendship I hasten to add but 'junket face recognition'), I could sense she was more wary than usual so I trod lightly with my questioning.

I've just re-read the transcript from that day and found barely anything personal in there apart from a quote about chocolate.

"*The last bag of choc I bought was Cadbury from London. I bought it for my mum it's the only thing she ever asks for. Fruit & Nut. Little miniature ones.*"

I clearly didn't peel back any layers that day. I remember leaving the room knowing that something was going on that I wasn't privy to. Even if I was, I probably would have been stopped from asking about it.

Two weeks later news broke that she'd adopted a baby boy called Jackson. My editor emailed to ask if she'd talked about it with me. When I stopped laughing at the thought that Charlize would casually drop this exclusive into my lap, I figured that the adoption might have been part of what had been going on that day. Or not. I don't know and won't pretend to. All I knew is that her usually fun demeanor was missing in action and I had to play it straight.

The story broke after I'd filed the copy so I had to rewrite the intro to include the one quote available about her now having a baby to look after and then make it fit seamlessly into our chat.

Charlize and I always got on well – but not too well. If you're getting on famously with a celebrity and they're asking endless questions about you and your life, then see this as a red flag. Celebrities generally don't care about the normals so see this for what it is: a cunning distraction technique.

It's clever on their part because it can lull the unsuspecting journalist into thinking they're special, which is hugely intoxicating but most importantly, from their point of view, it eats up precious time which is useful if the questions you're about to ask them are tricky or personal.

Unfortunately for the journalist it also puts you in a position where you have to be curt in order to move the interview along. You can't be too rude, but you must be firm.

A journalist friend of mine told me about an interview with a famous pop star turned reality show judge who spent most of their interview time complimenting her on her clothes, her engagement ring, and then asked lots of questions about her upcoming marriage. She couldn't be rude, but the clock was ticking and she felt uncomfortable about having to cut her off. Another TV star would talk endlessly about her cat and if you mentioned you have one too, she wanted to see pictures of it. This is all very well if you have an afternoon to spare but not within the confines of a 15-minute chat.

Stay alert. Once you realise what is going on, a polite but firm, “That’s great,” or, “Thanks!” followed by, “Let’s get down to business,” or, “I’d love to chat more but time is marching on,” followed by a question does the trick. Forge breezily ahead. No more cat or clothes talk. Not until you’ve got all you need.

Other times merely asking for an age can be a minefield (and no, I don’t always rely on the Internet to get this information as often it’s wrong). Actors generally don’t like to give away their ages for fear of being pigeon-holed. Usually I will say, “Do you mind if I ask you your age?” By which time I’ve asked the question but also have made myself seem extremely considerate. Nine times of ten it’s no big deal but sometimes it’s a huge deal and then you just move swiftly on.

Don’t be afraid to follow-up or challenge an answer two or three times if you think you’re not getting the pot of gold at the end of the rainbow. Instinct plays its part, but most journalists know when they’re being handed a vanilla-scented soundbite. That’s lovely if you need to freshen up your bathroom but it doesn’t make for interesting reading.

I've never had to grill a celebrity in the way that news reporters take on politicians but there have certainly been times when I know what I'm hearing is, how shall I say it, horseshit. Sometimes a nudge or two will elicit a better answer but often times you'll be shut down. That's okay. Move on. At least you tried. In a junket situation it's hard to warm up your subject sufficiently to allow them to relax fully (this is why we need more time!) so you can only do your best given the confines.

When I worked on teen and women's mags in the nineties, it wasn't unusual to spend a full day (or even two or three) hanging out with whoever it was you were profiling. You'd meet for dinner or lunch, watch their concert, visit the set, or stick around for the shoot, get VIP passes to whatever event it was they were promoting, travel with them on the plane or tour bus. This kind of unfettered access just doesn't happen as frequently now but in my humble opinion, it most definitely should. Stepping out of a limo with a human who is currently 'hot' (as I once did for a story) is simultaneously thrilling and terrifying, especially when the fans are teenage girls. Your hearing will never be the same again but that kind of front-of-line access is absolutely worth the late-life tinnitus.

As I'm editing this book, and as a juicy side note to this problem, I saw that there was an intense Twitter ripple from celebrity interviewers when Michaela Coel, the genius creator/writer/producer of *Chewing Gum* and *I May Destroy You*, revealed that she gave a writer from Vulture.com 14 hours of her time. The resulting article by E Alex Jung is fantastic.

This type of deep-dive celebrity interview would be so much better for everyone concerned if the journalist in question wasn't trying to shoehorn a cover story into mere minutes. It doesn't have to be that way all the time. For example, you don't need a lot of time to discuss a soap actor's upcoming storyline for a listings mag but being able to take a breath – and having the space to get deeper into your line of questioning – should be more of a given than it is right now.

But back to asking the hard questions. Many times, and particularly in the weekly market, interviews are paid for, and contracts drawn up that state quite clearly what the celebrity is expected to talk about. At that point you have licence to ask whatever it is you need, although sometimes you will find yourself in a battle with managers and PRs who hover like skittish undertakers taking umbrage at anything they deem too sensitive. Most times though, the negotiations will have happened ahead of time and everyone will know what to expect.

I remember the time I interviewed film-maker Patrick Moote for *Grazia UK* about his 2013 documentary, *UnHung Hero*, which looked at the importance of penis size.

The interview was on the phone as he was in the States while I was in London and we had a lot of ground to cover. In this instance there was no beating around the bush, I just had to go for it.

"We've never met but can you tell me everything about your small penis."

Part of what he said was this, "The amazing thing about the documentary, or 'cockumentary' as I call it, is that it made me realise that I'm a normal guy. I went to look for a series of remedies (pills, contraptions, exercises) to get bigger; I considered penis injection treatment in Papua New Guinea, and penis enlargement surgery in Korea, but ultimately learnt to accept myself. I know I'm on the lower side of average but that's okay."

So I suppose what I'm saying here is that when it comes to the way you ask your questions it's okay to talk about dicks, just don't be one.

HEADLINES:

How and when you ask a question is as important as the question you ask.

If a celebrity is over friendly realise that it's probably a distraction technique.

If you interview a child, always get permission from a parent or guardian.

Don't shy away from following up or getting into detail or emotion.

Most importantly, don't be a dick.

CHAPTER EIGHT

PEELING BACK A LAYER

A celebrity interview is in essence a conversation. An exchange of words between two people and a chance to shoot the breeze and kick back for a few minutes.

Oh, who am I kidding, it's so much more.

It's not exactly life or death but everybody involved has an agenda.

The studio needs to publicise their movie.

The producers need good press so they can make more money.

The star needs to look good in order to land more roles/advertising campaigns.

The publicists must deliver on behalf of their client.

And the publication or site you're writing for needs to generate clicks that can translate into ad sales.

In terms of the bigger picture it's important you understand this. I didn't think about my job in these terms for many years and while I'm not saying other agencies should drive your agenda, you need to be aware of who is expecting what and how you can deliver on your promise.

It needs to go well for a myriad of reasons, and not just because you think it looks good to post a photo of you snuggling up to a ridiculously attractive human who's been in hair and make-up for four hours, and therefore rendering you instantly less attractive.

You need good lines to take to your editor (meaning the best or most interesting aspect of the story), and the celebrity needs their project to fly so that they can buy themselves another beach-front property in Malibu or country pile in the Cotswolds.

It's a passive aggressive hug that takes mutual understanding from both sides to work.

I probably should have started the book with that line. Never mind. Sometimes a dropped intro can be a beautiful surprise.

Without a raft of well thought out questions at your disposal you're not going to get the best answers. I need you to think like a dentist: they use surgical instruments to extract teeth and your questions are one of the instruments you use to extract everything you need.

Now stop thinking like a dentist because that's gross, and many people quite possibly dislike them more than journalists.

When covering junkets, the questions you find yourself asking can get…now how do I put this without seeming too judgemental about the media sausage factory? Samey? Repetitive? Dull?

It's bad enough for the humble journalist so can you imagine being a famous person on the receiving end of the 387th ask of: "Why did you decide to take this role?"

Let's start with the basics and look at how to craft your questioning in order to keep your subject equally engaged and hopefully get to a point where you're able to peel back a layer, learn something new, and get a good story to boot.

The basics, like the proverbial bitch, are inherently snore inducing. But as I explained with Adrien Brody earlier, it's easy to get them wrong and if you do, the consequences can be brutal.

I'm not suggesting that you walk into a room, sit down opposite Meryl Streep and bark, "Name, age, place of birth," in her face. But whenever I interview a celebrity, always at the top of my list of questions I keep more or less the same scribbled note: *names, kid's names, ages, birth dates, campaign*?

This is to remind me to ask for those fiddly yet necessary details, usually at the end of the interview but sometimes during.

Unless it's going to ruin the flow of a particularly emotional story, I think it's perfectly okay to ask the celebrity to confirm the ages of their children, date of birth, or name spellings if they're ambiguous or unusual, as is often the case these days. You'd better ask while you have that person in front of you because they're in the best position to know.

"So, your baby is called Peppermint with a Y instead of an I, and a silent H after the P? Pheppermynt. Okay, great thanks."

If you don't check as you go, bear in mind as you talk that you may need to circle back for these crucial details later. Write the note on your hand, on the top of your notepad, or send yourself a push notification, I don't care how you do it just make sure you get the details correct.

When you sit down to compile your questions, always refer to your brief first. You need to hit all the required beats so make sure you include everything your editor requires.

The celebrity interviews I used to do for *OK!* magazine were unique in that everyone had an enormous amount of input (for reasons explained in an earlier chapter) and therefore the number of questions sometimes seemed never-ending. While you should use your judgement as to what you end up asking in the moment, the devil is in the detail and after doing so many baby chats, I now realise how much is involved in a good birth story. Frankly, the permutations of labour are endless and you have to ask everything because I tell you now, if you miss one tiny detail about the use of a ventouse or the contents of an overnight bag, that's going to be the one thing your editor will need you to answer.

This takes time. I remember once talking so long to Suzanne Shaw, formerly of reality pop group Hear'Say, about the birth of her second child Rafferty that myself, her partner, son, and newborn were left sitting in a south London location house long after our allotted time.

Darkness had fallen and we all agreed that it felt as if we'd broken into a stranger's house in order to have a cosy chat at their kitchen table.

When there are newborns, complicated birth stories, and glossy photographs involved, know that your day on set is going to run long every single time. Later, I'll dive deeper into the fun of doing interviews on shoot days but for now, let's stick to the questions.

Despite the mountains of technology out there, if I can, I still like to print out my questions so that I can scribble notes on them as I go. I find that a notepad or fat wedge of paper can be a nice steadying prop. You've probably figured out by now that I like a prop! I like to hold something and do a little newsreader paper shuffle. But again, that's just me.

Also, I get that you may not be able to afford to have your own printer (the price of ink is and has always been extortionate) or see printing questions as a waste of paper. Understandable. Many journalists now use only their phones or tablets and I do that sometimes too (especially when I run out of expensive printer ink). Just figure out what works best for you.

Be aware though that if you print out your questions and are holding what seems like a mountain of paper, it can be overwhelming for the interviewee. If I see so much as a flicker of fear on my subject's face I always tell them that it's not as much as it looks (when it probably is and so much more) and crack on before they have a chance to run away.

With all interviews I put in an enormous amount of research before separating the lines of questioning into different sections.

For example there will be the movie, TV show, or product/campaign launch as one section, then home life/family/children, fitness/health as another, their early life/backstory, or the latest scandal/headline/campaign.

Once I have everything clustered into sections, I look at my questions again.

If it's a book have I read the book and taken all I need from it?

Where are the gaps?

What are the personal details I've missed?

Will the order I've written them in enable the conversation to flow easily?

Is there a good balance of light and shade?

You don't want to go from the death of a spouse to: "What's your favourite smoothie?" No, no, no.

I see all my interviews in terms of a story arc. I want to go on a journey with this person and I want the reader to come with me.

I have written screenplays so maybe some of that comes into play, but I cannot bear to meander like a nosy bumblebee around a summer garden. I like to see the path my story is taking ahead of the interview and think on my feet during it if we happen to go off piste for whatever reason. This happens often because an interview is a conversation, but you will generally always need to pull focus and bring it back to your original line of questioning at some point.

As a side note I just want to say something about my use of the word 'story'. I'm no longer a news reporter and haven't been for a very long time now.

I was a reporter at the *Southend Evening Echo* from 1987 for three years and then for a while in 2005/2006 when I did shifts at *Media Guardian* but have worked in features for almost all my career.

News reporters report the news and are fact-based.

I tell stories that contain facts.

My speciality is celebrity profile pieces and I consider myself a storyteller every time I sit down to write them. I have journalist friends who I know will hate this description but that's not my concern. They can write their own book.

I see my features in terms of a story arc with a beginning, a middle, and an end. There are high moments and there are low moments. Ultimately, there is a journey.

Everyone knows who Drew Barrymore, Hugh Jackman, and Charlize Theron are, so I like to offer the reader something more than just a pedestrian stringing together of the facts.

When I set a scene, attempt to analyse a personality or craft a storyline for my piece, I'm doing more than just bashing out the words. I'm creating a world that hopefully entertains, informs, and also educates. I want the reader to feel some emotion and also enjoy the read over their Sunday morning croissants or morning commute. News stories are there to be economically informative; celebrity profiles require a different structure and tone.

So that's why I use the word story. As I say, lots of journalists hate it. I'm not one of them.

One of tricks with celebrity interviews is to appear to be asking questions that seem fresh even if they're not.

Your research will play into that, but you'll also need to think on your feet during the interview. Your questions are not just surgical instruments but also a road map to your story.

What, as a celebrity interviewer, can you tell me about this person that I do not know?

I always set out to find the unexpected and offer something new and you must do the same.

An example of one of the times I successfully did this was when I interviewed reality TV star and businesswoman Jessica Simpson in New York.

This was 2008 and I summed up where her career was at that point quite nicely in my profile for *Sunday Magazine*:

Packaged as the wholesome newlywed in her reality TV series with now ex-husband Nick Lachey, she went from successful early noughties pop star (part of the Britney/Christina era) to everyone's favourite dumb blonde (she thought buffalos actually had wings), to tabloid staple (following her divorce she had a high-profile relationship with musician John Mayer), and now she's re-invented herself as a country music artist.

By the time I got to sit down with Jessica and her pup Daisy, in the bar of the Ritz-Carlton Hotel in Manhattan, over a glass of white wine, I was curious as to who I was about to meet.

Surely she couldn't be as goofy as the headlines suggested?

In my transcript I wrote these stream-of-consciousness colour notes. Here they are verbatim:

Daisy at the beginning of the interview – girly blonde moment. Studious, quiet, thoughtful but sunny. Level-headed all in black, gold bangles long, gold earrings tiny – greeted dog with squeaky voice – warm hug at the end. Open to all questions, exhausted after a day of interviews in dark room, glass of Pinot Grigio, roman strap heels.

This was written just after I'd left the bar and described like this in the copy:

I'm waiting in the bar of the Ritz-Carlton hotel in Manhattan, New York, talking to one of her assistants, who is holding her perfectly coiffed Maltese cross poodle, Daisy.

Ever the obedient pup, Daisy is sitting placidly in the crook of his arm like a hand puppet until Jessica rounds the corner, shrieks at a level hitherto unknown to man, before showering her pet with a million kisses.

'Hey, Daisy baby, how was your walk?' she exclaims in her southern accent. 'How are you my darlin', look at you!'

And on it goes, the high-pitched tone almost shattering the glassware until Daisy, unmoved, is escorted back to her suite.

Only while being simultaneously introduced to me and a nicely chilled glass of Pinot Grigio, does her voice return to a normal pitch.

Sloppy journalism is often just a series of assumptions and stock phrases. I'm mindful of this and try to avoid them at all costs (especially BS sexist ones). I hate the fact I used the phrase ‘dumb blonde’ in the copy, even if it was more than ten years ago. Note to self: moving forward, do better.

I like to think we’re evolving when it comes to our use of language in print; I haven’t heard the phrase ‘gymslip mum’ in years, thank goodness. However, there is a still a long way to go, especially when you look at certain online news sites and the clichés they use to string together the most tenuous of stories.

There had to be something more to Jessica.

Thankfully, my interview revealed another layer when I asked about the day-to-day running of her business empire. I’d read a few lines during my research about how much her company was making and I was intrigued. It’s not easy running a profitable company, so how was she doing it? Was it her or a host of faceless suits?

Her answer to that question showed her in a different light entirely and was ultimately picked up by other outlets.

This is what she said when I asked her about the Jessica Simpson Collection, which later became the first celebrity-owned clothing line in history to earn $1 billion in annual sales.

Turnover is robust and believe it or not, she oversees every major decision.

"I'm very hands on," she explains, while also giving credit to her parents, Joe and Tina Simpson, for being instrumental in the day-to-day running of the company. "I'm hoping that the business will outlive me and I plan on making this – and I don't care if it sounds like my hopes are too high – a business model based on Ralph Lauren, or a Michael Kors type of line."

With such lofty aspirations, it's no surprise to learn that the company takes up a large chunk of her time.

"I think people would be surprised to know what I do on a daily basis – I don't just date guys!" she laughs. "I actually work really hard."

And that translates into a schedule that would make most people go weak at the knees.

"We have at least three approval meetings a week because with fashion, you have to go with seasons," she says, explaining that she's just approved her Spring 2009 range. "I attend board meetings and keep any eye on everything. I have to, it's my name and I want it to be represented as close to who I am."

Is she comfortable in that world?

"It's definitely different," she concedes. "But it's a very lucrative business for me and that's one of the reasons that making this record was a lot easier; I didn't have to worry about anything financially. That helps as an artist because you're not trying to create music you think will be commercial – that's what I'd been doing for so long. Looking back, I don't think I was comfortable doing pop music, now I feel I'm ahead of the curve."

This from the same Jessica Simpson who famously thought that 'chicken of the sea' was actually chicken and not tuna.

Overall, I like this interview a lot because for me it did what I always try to do. It peeled back a layer.

I discovered new things about her and so did the reader.

It's not always that easy. Reading back my transcript notes for an interview I did with Keanu Reeves I can see that I'm trying to peel back a tough little layer with this exchange:

Me: *Tell me something about you that would surprise people.*

Keanu: *Just like that*?

Me: *Yes, just like that.*

Keanu: *That's a hard one, I don't know what would surprise someone.*

Me: *Do you play Monopoly, bake cakes – maybe you should? That would be surprising.*

Keanu: *I'm sorry, I can't help you out there.*

Bake cakes? Monopoly? Gawd, I completely lost the plot there.

Keanu was a hard nut to crack but over the course of our interview I did, after mentioning I was coming up to 40, enquire if he had any advice about getting older. Cue multiple funnies about the onset of creaky bones and unwanted nose hair.

Asking someone to "Tell me something about yourself that would surprise people", is a little on the nose. I'll only use it as a fall-back question if I feel as if I haven't got enough anecdotally, or if there's a giant lull for some reason. Sometimes it works and you're handed a golden nugget, other times, they just "can't help you out there".

There's another aspect to peeling back a layer that's worth mentioning, and that is sometimes, there might not be another layer.

The business angle from Jessica Simpson was a beautiful reveal because it went so against type but sometimes there's nothing else. Celebrities are after all just people. They don't have all the answers. Sometimes they're just an extremely bland canvas.

I'm not going to name the people I thought were one dimensional and tedious. To be honest, it didn't happen often as nine times out of ten if you're doing a good job – and this is your job – you will always find something fresh, exciting, and new. On occasion however, you will dig and dig and find nothing but a big, beautiful empty hole.

That's when you'll trot out the standard questions about diet and fitness, invasion of privacy and quite possibly: "What's your favourite smoothie?"

It's understandable that you want these feted, carb-free super humans to somehow have all the answers and be better than the rest of us but remember, they're also just regular people too. They are regular people who in most cases have a standout talent that's been elevated through the lottery of life, have good genes, flatter stomachs, bigger muscles, and get more press than you.

Don't be upset sometimes if you are disappointed.

But don't let that stop you trying to peel back the layers. More often than not, you will find something that piques your interest, and chances are if you're interested, then you've also hooked your audience.

Surprises are often uncovered. I'm always intrigued as to what random fact I might stumble upon seemingly out of nowhere. Some of them, many years on, I remember well.

I remember Julianna Margulies, from *ER*, telling me that she used to work in a bar in Tenerife. Interesting to me because that's where my family lived for a long time.

Sharlto Copley, the actor from *The A-Team* reboot and *District 9*, talked to me about founding what was essentially the MTV of South Africa.

Or Steve Carell waxing lyrical about how he toured Glasgow in the mid-nineties with his improv group eating haggis and sampling the local beers.

There's always something. Get your peeler out, add it to your toolbox which contains your story roadmap and use it along with the rest of your surgical instruments.

If we carry on like this, we'll have enough weapons to get to Zelda's lair, and I bet she's got an interesting back story too.

HEADLINES:

Always try to find something new.
Craft your questions to get the most out of the interview.
Think about the arc of your story.
Remember to hit all the beats required by the brief.
Don't be afraid to fact check in the moment.

CHAPTER NINE

NEVER ASSUME A THING

Because of the nature of the job you will almost always have an opinion of the person you're about to interview. People form views, it's human nature.

More often than not, though, whatever opinion you have in advance of the interview will prove completely and utterly wrong once you've actually met them.

The exception is obviously Ryan Gosling. You and everyone else on the planet will love him. It's the law in Hollywood so don't bother to put in an appeal.

It's actually incredibly difficult to walk into a room with zero expectations of an extremely famous person. It's not just their personality, it's also their physicality. They almost always look exactly like that person you identify with from that hit show or movie. It's fascinating but as I explained earlier when talking about Jessica Simpson, unless you can turf out those preconceived ideas you probably won't be able to get beyond the surface gloss and do a good interview.

I was lucky enough in LA to have the chance to interview Jason Alexander, who played George Costanza in *Seinfeld*, one of my favourite comedies.

Seinfeld, a US sitcom starring Jerry Seinfeld, Julia Louis-Dreyfus, Jason Alexander, and Michael Richards, ran for nine years from 1989. The 1998 finale drew in 76 million viewers in the US and has since gone on to make billions of dollars in syndication.

George has small man complex. He is a pedant, a bit creepy, and an opportunist.

George also looks a lot like the actor Jason Alexander. It was almost impossible for me not to walk into the room and like Jerry himself yell, "George!"

This is what he said when I explained my gut reaction to seeing him in person.

He was pretty cool about it.

"I'm recognised as George Costanza everywhere I go. It's been ten years since Seinfeld ended but I came to terms with the show's success a long time ago. As it started to become a big hit, I realised that I could either resent it or get to the more mature place of saying, 'What an amazing thing to have in my life and not everybody gets one.'"

And he also amusingly said this, *"I don't know that I'd want a George in my life. I loved playing him but on a real level, I don't know. Having said that, I haven't travelled anywhere that people haven't been happy to see George, which is a huge thing. Acting is such a self-serving career, there are times you sit there and go, 'I should do something for the world,' but what happens with a show like Seinfeld is that I've met people who've said, 'We lost a child, we lost a parent, I was going through chemo, I thought we would never laugh again but you guys got us through,' and you know, that's pretty good.*"

But he's not George Costanza. Jason's real name is Jay Greenspan. He's a married father of two and besides acting he's also a successful director.

Finding out about Jay Greenspan was a lot more interesting than having a chat with his *Seinfeld* character. But I'll be honest, it was tough getting past that adorable George Costanza face of his.

Another big deal at the time was an interview I did with Tom Anderson, who in 2007 was the king of the Internet.

He co-founded the social network MySpace in 2003 with his partner Chris DeWolfe, and then went on to sell it three years later for £512 million to Fox Media, which at the time was ground-breaking.

Meeting him at his offices in Los Angeles felt like meeting the Wizard of Oz.

Tom was a mysterious figure to say the least. Who was I going to find behind the velvet curtain?

And what was this brand-new concept of a 'social network' that had installed him in place as its overlord?

Remember this was pre-Facebook, or at least Facebook wasn't anything like the behemoth it is now. MySpace was then both the present and the future.

The MySpace building was large and imposing and there was a lot of security to get through. I remember doing a bit of a Betty White bag fumble as I was led into his office.

Turns out, Tom, who was everyone's friend, was a normal guy who loved his mum.

He said, "*It's not really true to call me a nerd or a computer geek. It wouldn't bug me if you did but if people look at me as the tech guy who created MySpace, it's completely inaccurate. I was way more technical when I was a teenager because back then I was writing programmes, but I didn't write a line of code for MySpace. That's not what I do here at all – I'm more the creative side. But my programming background helps me to understand what the programmers are doing even though they're light years ahead of me. From a technical standpoint, the basic framework of MySpace is very simple but when you scale it out to millions of people, it gets incredibly complicated.*"

And also this, "*My mum is basically a saint. She was a pre-school teacher, but she retired when I was growing up. She now helps problem kids and gets paid $8 an hour to do a super important job. It's ridiculous how little her pay is but she won't take anything from me. I say, 'Don't you want a house or a car?' and she says: 'No I'm fine.' She doesn't want anything.*"

He also shared with me that he hadn't gone on holiday since starting MySpace.

"*That whole distinction or the concept of a vacation doesn't really resonate with me. I don't think of how I've got to get away, it's just not in my nature. I'm not sitting here waiting for the weekend or wishing I could take off for two weeks. I do mellow stuff on the weekends like watching movies, shopping, or sitting around the house but I always tend to check in on the site. I'm never really away from the job.*"

However, I can see from his Instagram account now that he hasn't stopped going on holiday since he left the company. And good for him, who wouldn't love a giant bank balance and the opportunity to do the same.

Celebrity interviews are in a way a lottery. You really never know what's waiting for you.

Someone who you think may be a posh, fashion plate, and a bit aloof ahead of your interview could surprise you by offering to make a cup of tea as you settle into the sofa in their hotel suite.

That would be Keira Knightley, who I met at the Ham Yard Hotel in London, in 2013, while she was publicising *Begin Again*, in which she starred with Mark Ruffalo.

She was incredibly nice. Friendly, well-spoken, and not in any way aloof. She had an ask-me-anything attitude which always makes for a more interesting interview.

And she's not a natural fashion plate either. "*I'm scruffy and have always been scruffy. Obviously, I'm not today but somebody has been hired to make me look not scruffy! I was never into fashion when I was younger, so fashion is a world I find myself in having never meant to be here,*" she told me.

And in case you were wondering, her tea-making skills were exemplary.

Essentially, what you're looking to do is avoid cliché. Assumptions are based on cliché and cliché is the killer of creativity.

If you want to brush up on your clichés check out the side bar of a popular daily news website, and other outlets. They talk about celebrities being braless (this is such a weird fixation and so wrong, please stop), celebrities pouring their curves into whatever it is they're wearing, using their never-ending pins to step out with their squad/beau/crew/bae, showcasing their baby bump/side-boob/under-boob/washboard abs (which nine times out of ten are non-existent), flaunting their weight loss/weight gain, displaying their glossy, flowing tresses and my personal favourite, 'stunning' people with, no, not their futuristic fifties sci-fi stun guns, but dazzling beauty.

I think unless you choose to write for a publication which uses this style of descriptive vernacular try to avoid clichés at all costs. And if pushed, I'll say this while wearing a bra and again later while not wearing a bra.

Also important is that you should never assume you know what someone is going to say. You may be asking the celebrity to comment on something that they've talked about many times before. They may have a perfectly manicured PR line to share but sometimes you'll get something you didn't expect.

Many times my heart has sunk at the thought of asking yet another pedestrian question about privacy, health, fitness, typecasting, family, or love life.

There are times when you may find yourself answering the question in your head as you say it out loud. But like the urge to check Twitter just before bedtime, it's an urge you need to fight.

Nine times out of ten you'll get the party line but sometimes you'll hear something surprising. Those are the moments you live for as a celebrity journalist, especially one who covers junkets.

The truth is that most celebrities are coached within an inch of their lives ahead of their press tour. This is why you hear them say the same thing in the room, on the radio, on the morning TV sofa and online.

Their soundbites have been put to a committee and rehearsed.

It's a difficult situation for a journalist because you can only do so much in the given time and nobody wants to write the same story as the 17 people before you or the 17 people after you.

Sometimes, given the junkets can be a sausage factory it's hard not to get bogged down by the 'What is it all for?' of it all.

This is when you have to dig deep and look for a glimmer of something good.

Throwing out a weary sigh of a question will more often than not garner an answer so dull you could hang it over England and call it summer.

But making assumptions ahead of time will only make the situation worse. And the bigger the star the more assumptions you might have.

I interviewed Colin Farrell in 2013 in London ahead of the release of the film *Winter's Tale*, which also starred former *Downton Abbey* actress Jessica Brown Findlay.

Back in the day Colin Farrell had what the tabloids call a 'bad boy' image. A good ten years before I met him, Colin was regular tabloid fodder. Irish born and with the kind of swagger that only a movie star can pull off, he dated Playboy models, went on wild drink and drug binges, and even starred in his own sex tape. He entered rehab in December 2005.

If ever there was a man to make an assumption about it was Colin Farrell.

Maybe because he was knocking on 40 or because he was now a dad, the man I met was nothing like the man I'd read about.

He told me his favourite romantic movie was *Tootsie*: "*How romantic was Charles Durning in that film when he gives Tootsie the ring*?"

He was polite and softly spoken. I was knocked off guard a little. Not because movie stars aren't good at being all the above (acting!) but because of the giant bag of assumptions I'd tried not to bring – but clearly had – into the room with me.

Bad boy? More like hopeless romantic.

This is from my overs (the quotes that didn't get used in the story for the Australian *Telegraph's Sunday Style magazine*):

"*One of the things I love about Los Angeles is the way it's between desert and an ocean, and then the hills and mountains the nature is extraordinary. I do miss the walking and the more communal aspect of life in London or Dublin, but I believe in the magic of nature and love and kindness. I love getting out and hill walking and having a gander. I live by Griffith Park and there are miles of trails and there's never anyone around except for falcons and hummingbirds*."

Hummingbirds?

The only other person I've ever discussed hummingbirds with is reality TV star Spencer Pratt for *OK!* magazine in 2017, who was busy feeding his when his wife Heidi went into labour.

But back to Colin.

I was so intrigued by the man sat in front of me, wearing a suit so sharp I think it was made of Dorothy Parker, that I asked him what he would say to his younger self if he could travel back 20 years in time? (The question also worked very well for the movie which is all about time travel.)

He laughed and said, "*I wouldn't listen to anything I had to say, it would all fall on deaf ears. Honestly, I don't know what wisdom I would be able to impart because everything I've been through has led me to this point. I'm alive, I'm healthy, and I feel very grateful, so I don't know. If the me today met me from 20 years ago, the me today would be so blanked by my younger self. And frankly, I wouldn't want to spend too much time with the me from 20 years ago, he would bore the pants off me*!"

Again, I think that I met Dad Colin and not Bad Boy Colin but I was expecting to meet Bad Boy Colin but that was okay because I got to meet an actual person and not a headline.

I also asked him what was so special about having children and his eyes misted over. I think that for him being a dad has taken off the pressure of being a movie star. At least that's what I got from this answer.

On his kids: "*It's nice that everything doesn't have to be about you any more. It's a relief – the world is bigger than you instantly and also, it's just a lot of fun. Little people are really cool and interesting and filled with potential and you just wanted that potential to find its own path. I love hanging out with them.*"

His hotel in London overlooked the Thames. I commented on the location which was truly breathtaking and he told me that he'd been for a long walk along the river.

Nothing remotely bad about any of that.

The director James Cameron has a reputation for being arrogant. The best example of this is probably the moment he won the Best Director Oscar for *Titanic* in 1998, when he got to the podium, held his gong aloft and declared, "I'm the king of the world!"

In 2011 I was invited to the Fox lot in Los Angeles to watch footage of *Titanic* in 3D. We were told that James Cameron would be present to introduce the screening and I was very excited because the Fox lot is another of my favourite studio lots.

It's where *Three Coins in the Fountain*, *Carousel*, *Bus Stop*, *Cleopatra*, *The King and I*, *The Sound of Music*, *Hello, Dolly!*, *M.A.SH. Big*, *Broadcast News*, and *Speed*, and so many more were filmed. They also have amazing topiary and there's nothing better than a hedge shaped like a horse.

The first time I visited I managed to peel myself away from the press pack just so that I could wander around by myself and soak up the atmosphere in a sort of weird movie reverie.

Eventually a security guard in a golf cart, who had circled me twice, asked me what I was doing and when I told him he just smiled which suggested it had happened before. Starry-eyed movie lovers soaking up the rarefied air. He kindly told me that I wasn't allowed to wander the studio lot by myself and directed me back to the car park. Still, it was nice while it lasted.

After we watched the *Titanic* 3D footage which was pretty bloody amazing – and this is from someone who gets nauseous wearing the glasses – we headed to a patio area outside the screening room for a buffet lunch.

By chance I found myself filing along the lunch line next to Mr Cameron. We had a chat about the footage and then we did that getting-food-in-line thing where you exchange plates (sandwiches in this case), and then he asked me if I wanted a packet of chips (that's crisps for those you in the UK) and I said, "Yes I would." So he reached over and handed me a packet of Doritos and on and on it went in a non-arrogant, non-threatening, pleasant lunch line experience kind of way, until our plates were full and we peeled off to eat at different tables.

I'm sharing this because it's easy to hear one thing about a person and think that this is them. Nobody is so one dimensional that they're only ever what you hear or read in a headline.

Well…hold up…actually that's not strictly true, your honour. Sometimes you do hear things about A-listers and they do end up being near to what you may have heard.

Which brings me to 007 himself, Daniel Craig.

His reputation is that he is difficult to interview; the assumption being that he does not particularly like or want to be interviewed. He rarely does them and generally refuses to discuss anything too personal. This can be a little scary as you never know how, what, or where the line is that you cannot cross.

This is an excerpt from writer John Naughton in a rather brilliant interview with Daniel Craig for *GQ* in 2012:

Before long, you end up discussing the difficulty of interviewing Daniel Craig. You end up discussing other people's difficulties interviewing Daniel Craig. You end up discussing a particularly disastrous encounter with Jonathan Ross a few years ago, when, in the course of promoting Casino Royale follow-up Quantum Of Solace, he gave the impression that given the choice between Wossy's leather sofa or being water boarded in Guantanamo it would be a window seat on the next rendition flight to Cuba for Mr Craig.

*"I'm just not very good at it," he recalls with a wry grimace, the memory of his tongue-tied, magic-free encounter with Ross still obviously fresh in his mind. "I can't do that. I don't have jazz hands," he laughs, throwing out his large mitts in the manner of the Broadway song-and-dance make-'em-laugh merchant he most patently is not. "I wish I did have f***ing jazz hands, but I don't. I can't do it," he continues, enumerating the reasons why he often comes across badly on chat shows.*

"I'm a really bad liar. I don't have those pat things to say. Well, I have a schtick; everyone has a schtick. But if I don't feel it, I can't turn it on."

His press tour for *Spectre* in 2015 was famous for him saying this about James Bond. *"I'd rather break this glass and slash my wrists... I'm over it at the moment. We're done. All I want to do is move on."*

The furore that followed that dramatic comment was tumultuous. But I do wonder given his inability to do 'jazz hands' is that he's concerned that his lack of filter will ultimately get him to say things he just does not want to share?

Any tentpole press tour is gruelling. Making the films themselves is gruelling. Yes movie stars are well paid for it but by the time the "I'd rather break this glass and slash my wrists" comment was made he was probably heartily sick of talking about Bond, thinking about Bond, and inhabiting the world of Bond. Not everyone is equipped to do press well. And even those who can often struggle with its repetitive nature.

I met Daniel Craig during a roundtable interview for the movie *Cowboys & Aliens* at a ranch called Paws Up, in Montana.

The location was absolutely stunning (they don't call Montana 'open sky country' for nothing). During the roundtable he turned around another journalist's flip-cam ("Am I going to end up on some website? Can I turn it away then? I don't like lenses."), covered up a tattoo on his arm that said 'A time for timelessness' when asked about it ("Just for me and nobody else"), and declined to take a photo with one of the journalists at the end of the interview. "*I was hoping it was about paper and not photographs*."

His answers were short. He explained why he wouldn't talk about his private life. "*My private life is my private life and as I get on, I get more and more private*."

I can see from my transcript that the most he had to say on any subject was about the newspaper hacking scandal, but he was also funny. When asked about his free time he said this, "*I never have any free time. If I do have any free time, I just spend time with friends and family, just do that, the normal stuff, I don't have any hobbies I can tell you about. I don't go fishing or sew. Some needlepoint at the weekend*". [Laughs.]

Essentially, he was exactly as I'd been led to believe, and it probably didn't help that he followed Harrison Ford, who is about as laid back as an actor can be sitting upright in a chair.

I would like the chance to interview Daniel Craig in a more relaxed environment or a one-to-one situation as I think things might play out differently. Or maybe not?

But I promise not to ask him about his tattoo. Although that's me assuming he won't want to talk about it.

Who knows, it may be different next time?

HEADLINES:

Never assume anything about anyone.
Assumptions can, and will, weigh you down.
Take as you find, your story will be more interesting.
Interview the person in front of you, not the headline.
If what you assume turns out to be true, use it as part of your story.

CHAPTER 10

ROLLING WITH THE PUNCHES

"*Lisa, choose a bagel. Anything you want.*"

Legendary talk show host Larry King had agreed to meet me at his bakery in Beverly Hills to talk all things bagels for *The Guardian*.

He owned a 50% stake in The Original Brooklyn Water Bagel Company franchise and was feeling generous.

Now, I was brought up on bagels as befits my Jewish heritage, so they don't generally faze me (just my waistline). Our family were eating bagels before the rest of the hipster world was eating bagels. Bagels are my comfort zone.

However, there's a big difference between the long-gone Jewish deli in Westcliff-on-Sea where my dad used to drive us to every weekend to buy bags of plain and onion bagels, and Larry's theme park steroid of a bagel bakery.

The choice in my hometown deli was minimal but everything we bought from that tiny shop situated opposite the station was delicious. It was a social club of sorts; lots of laughter and conversation with my dad, David, holding court. He would make the owners, his friends, and regulars laugh while we waited for the bagels, chopped liver, chopped herring, and rollmop to be bagged up.

Cut to 30 years later and I'm standing in a deli in Beverly Hills with a well-known TV host and I'm having a full-on bread panic.

Dig deep, Lisa, I thought, dig deep. Connect to your roots. Use that childhood experience to navigate you through this enormous billboard of a menu with its bewildering array of fillings, toppings, and combinations.

Suddenly racing through my head is the debate that has spanned generations of Marks family members and seems to be without conclusion.

Is it spelled bagel or beigel?

Is it pronounced bay-gall or bye-gel?

Not now, Lisa, no one cares. Focus. You can do this!

Larry's bagels had names like 'Jersey Boy' and 'the Williamsburg' and came with avocado, jalapeños, peanut butter, speciality cream cheese, and scallions. Huh?

I was floundering. Between the panic of finding parking in Beverly Hills, the anticipation of meeting TV ledge Larry, and choosing a complicated bagel my brain froze. I was felled by a boiled breakfast food.

Larry stepped in. "Try the salt bagel, no butter, with cream cheese, and smoked salmon. They scoop out the middle so it's not as fattening. You'll love it – but you'll be drinking water for the rest of the day."

"Good grief, Larry, what are you doing to my bagel?", I shouted inwardly.

"Er, ok…" I replied, outwardly.

In everyday life a salted bagel would almost certainly be my last choice of bagel. Cream cheese and smoked salmon I can eat from here until Christmas. Sorry, Passover.

But great big chunks of salt crystals as sprinkles, no thank you. Scooping out the middle? Isn't that a crime against bread (the Olsen twins do the same, apparently. I only know that because they told Oprah Winfrey and not me).

But this wasn't normal life. This was an interview with Larry King at his bagel emporium in 90210.

Professional hat on, it was time to roll with the punches.

I ate the scooped out salted bagel with cream cheese and smoked salmon.

And I will never eat another.

The thirst, the thirst! Oi vey, the thirst!

But when you get a celebrity away from the restraints of a junket, in to 'real life' or as close to it as you can, just about anything can happen. And you know what, it's a lot of fun when you do.

After greeting the well-heeled locals, one of which turned out to be Larry's childhood friend from Brooklyn, we sat in a side-booth which featured a microphone in his honour.

The interview was a hoot, if public. I remember stressing about picking up what Larry was saying on my Dictaphone over the buzzing diner din.

Larry held court and was open and frank. He also asked me a lot of questions, mostly about Piers Morgan, who had been announced as his successor on *CNN*. Larry later went on to host an online talk show on *Ora TV*.

I was a freelance commissioning editor on *The Mirror's Saturday TV* magazine for a couple of years and Piers Morgan was then the paper's editor. While my day-to-day concern was television, I was in the office in Canada Tower, east London, when the planes hit the World Trade Centre on 9/11, and that's my overriding memory of that time.

Piers Morgan divides opinion like no other. It should absolutely be noted that he left *The Mirror* under a dark and stormy cloud, a couple of years after I'd left in the normal way to move to *Media Guardian*. But before Twitter, before his vexatious obsession with Meghan Markle, his rollercoaster of a relationship with Trump, and weird revulsion of vegan sausage rolls, my personal experience of him wasn't in any way as divisive. He was most definitely a showman who enjoyed strutting around the newsroom making jokes and checking in on the different desks but he was also an editor who was passionate about the job. The pressure was on to produce a great newspaper every day and people worked extraordinarily long hours and were magnificently dedicated to their jobs.

Overall, I enjoyed my time on *The Mirror*. It was tough but I learnt a lot. Piers made sure that everyone knew they were appreciated with congratulatory group emails and often said thank you for work that was done over and above expectation. Not every editor does that, believe me.

He also memorably ordered us all to leave our desks to watch England play Argentina during the 2002 World Cup, telling us (via email) that if our line managers didn't let us decamp to the bar he'd booked out for the game, they'd be sacked (or something along these lines). Hence, the entire office spent a boozy afternoon in a nefarious drinking hole in Canary Wharf cheering on our lads. It was an old-school popularity chess move and it worked.

Pretty much what I've written above is what I told Larry, when he asked. He seemed surprised that I didn't go straight for the kill. I had no reason to.

This is what he told me of his successor: "*It's like watching your mother-in-law go over the cliff in your new car. There are days I miss it and days I don't. I watch Piers sometimes, he's fine.*"

I love that he managed to get a mother-in-law gag in there somehow. He also told me a joke.

What did the chicken say to the egg after having sex?

Well, we finally have the answer to the age-old question!

One of his cronies laughed and said, "That's funny. Keep 'em coming!"

Once I'd settled into the vibe of Larry's corner table of camaraderie, coffee, and comedy I was able to enjoy the interview. And he was a good interviewee, which is unusual for someone who is used to asking the questions.

His view of the Brooklyn Bagel Bakery was seen through rose-coloured glasses. It appeared to me to be more of an homage to his roots than a business decision. He was settling an old score or putting the past right somehow.

He told me, "*My father died when I was nine and a half, I moved from a poor neighbourhood into a middle-income neighborhood where I was the poorest kid. While my friends* *had $20, I would have $5. I had to go to a camp that was free, NYC bought my first pair of glasses, we were on relief for two years. I romanticise it but there were a lot of unhappy days in Brooklyn when I felt inferior to the friends around me because I didn't have that money.*"

And I really connected with what he said when I asked him about why he wanted to be a journalist, "*I was always curious about everything. That's what got me the opportunity. Diversity would be my middle name. I'm just as interested in that waitress as the president. I never lost that – you don't want to sit next to me on an airplane. The less I know about a subject the happier I am. How a building gets to be a building, how a movie gets to be made. I'm more interested in the writer than the book. I'm fascinated by actors.*"

Larry, you are my kindred spirit in almost everything but choice of bagel.

It was a one-off kind of interview and I loved it.

My second time around interviewing Miranda Kerr was also a roll with the punches kind of deal.

I drove to Palm Springs to interview Miranda, who was shooting for David Jones, the Australian department store. The interview appeared in the Australian *Telegraph's Sunday Magazine* in July 2011.

Palm Springs is where the beautiful people zip off to for the weekend and have an impossibly gorgeous time floating around their pool on a flamingo inflatable, mixing sundowner cocktails, later dining at a modern-fusion restaurant. There's a lot of money, cachet, and old-school Hollywood heft attached to the place.

This shoot took place at the luxurious Parker Hotel and I remember gliding around the grounds trying to soak up as much colour as I could for the story.

I felt as if I was in the pilot episode of a mid-century Netflix drama. On the croquet lawn, the hotel staff were dressing a chuppah (a traditional Jewish canopy) for a wedding that was due to take place later that day. I watched them methodically set out lines of folding chairs, before catching sight of a petite cellist setting up her music stand. It was divine.

But work called and I was invited into Miranda's inner sanctum. She was wearing a white hotel robe and all manner of shoot activity was happening around her.

I felt very comfortable as Miranda had asked for me specifically after the success of our interview the previous year. It's always nice to return for the sequel.

Here's how I opened the piece:

Dressed in a white robe, her hair pulled back in a casual knot, Miranda Kerr gazes out through a patio door onto the garden below. From here, she could easily be posing for the cover of a Danielle Steel novel.

In fact, she's working, and patiently waiting for her hair and make-up artists to finish yet another look for today's photo shoot.

The Aussie supermodel looks every inch the professional, immune to the fuss going on around her.

But perhaps the thing keeping her so calm isn't the pretty garden or the fact she's done this a thousand times before. Maybe it's because, among the hubbub, in her arms is her six-month-old son, Flynn.

Reading that back I probably wouldn't reference Danielle Steel again. I don't know why I did in the first place as she's never been a point of reference to me but there you go.

What I'd established here is that she'd just given birth but what I wasn't explicit about was that Miranda was also breast-feeding her six-month-old.

As we sat down to the do the chat Miranda started breast-feeding Flynn. This was a first for me during an interview. I've seen my friends breastfeed, but no one has ever breastfed more or less naked in front of me while I was asking them questions.

Roll with the punches.

My brain had to quickly adjust and let me make this clear, it was lovely, beautiful, and intimate, but it was also a surprise.

This is how I referenced her breastfeeding in the story:

Despite a demanding schedule, the 28-year-old from Gunnedah manages to stay enviably serene. After a few more shots, she takes the opportunity to feed Flynn again, while also feeding herself a plate of salmon and spinach, and a side of fries. "I need the carbs," she says.

In short, I didn't tell the whole story at all.

I didn't describe me sitting in a chair opposite Miranda, who was picking at food from the side table, white robe hanging open, baby Flynn at her breast.

At times she would stop talking to me and rearrange Flynn and softly say, "*I love you, I love you, my little boy.*"

Yes, it was distracting but wow, what a privilege to be part of such an intimate moment between a mother and child.

These days, just a few short years later, it's more acceptable to be brutally honest about many once taboo subjects, one of which was breastfeeding. If it happened again, I'd probably do it all differently (or maybe that's my women's celebrity weekly head talking, because if anyone does a baby chat for that market you literally learn everything from the way the sperm swam up the vaginal canal to what the midwife had for breakfast).

But seriously, I have to ask myself writing this chapter and reviewing the entire scene that maybe on this occasion I'd only rolled with half a punch?

Whatever, it was clear that I needed to go along with the tone that Miranda set and as you can imagine, I did. There was no way I was going to jump to my feet in outrage and crash out of the room, my delicate sensibilities having been so roundly stomped upon (again, I have to make clear that they weren't).

The interview, as I described in an earlier chapter about killer questions, made the front pages of the newspapers as well as the cover of the magazine, so it was a success. Miranda is easy to be around and it was a great day.

I reset my brain, absorbed the energy in the room, and got on with the job at hand.

On a completely different day, *Closer* magazine in the UK sent me to interview Janice Dickinson, who bills herself as the world's first supermodel, for a 'naked shoot'.

She was part of the original judging panel on *America's Next Top Model* and also appeared in the UK reality TV show *I'm A Celebrity – Get Me Out of Here!* in November 2007. Christopher Biggins won, but she was runner up and hugely popular with the viewing audience.

The shoot, in July 2010, was due to take place at her Brentwood home in Los Angeles which was high in the Hollywood Hills and I cannot lie, it was madness from start to finish.

It wasn't so much roll with the punches as get in a ring with Ali and do your best to stay alive.

Before I tell this story, which required every ounce of instinct, tact, and journalistic wit that I possessed, I want to make it clear that this is by no means a blasé attempt to belittle Janice or make her look ridiculous. I hope it doesn't. I liked her a lot. She is a unique lady and I found her utterly fascinating.

On this particular day she was grappling with various emotional issues and myself and the team from *Closer* walked straight into the middle of them.

I connected to her as a woman who has also been through many stages of life alone. When you're a journalist, you can't just switch that stuff off. Your empathy can be a great tool and you should use it when you can. Janice got under my skin.

For example, this is a part of an email I wrote to a friend while I was transcribing the tape a few days later. I say, '*...transcribing Janice Dickinson's tape has made me tearful. Especially when she starts crying about her dog and then sobs: "I'm not that crazy bitch you see on TV, I'm a nice person." *WAIL**'

Babs (my mother and, if you recall, a close friend of one Kimberly Kardashian) wrote to me around the time I was writing my story to say that she'd just watched Janice on a UK reality TV show.

She emailed this rather amusing summation (her email subject line was: That Bloody Woman: *Just watching* Come Dine with Me *with Janice Dickinson. What a crazy bore and chasing Calum Best who was not at all interested in her. How you managed to handle her I don't know, my hat goes off to you, Lisa.*

Thanks, Mum.

Funny right? Well, not entirely.

My reply was this, *When you watch it just remember that a fragile and lonely single mum who is going through the menopause is underneath all that mouth and snarkiness.*

Seen through an empathetic eye, you can elevate a story from snark to sharp.

Usually an at-home shoot is not done at home. Celebrities, quite rightly, don't want a journalist and crew trampling through their private space, and a location house is booked. Not today. We were at Janice's family home that she shared at the time with her two grown-up children Nathan, who was then 23, and 16-year-old Savannah (neither of whom were around that day).

This was the brief: *The idea is to get her to open up about her physical imperfections and what's driven her on an emotional level to do something about them by having surgery, treatments etc. and also, to find out what it's like being an older woman in the world of modelling and TV.*

Janice had agreed to be shot naked and our photographer that day was the brilliant Simon Perry and the genius stylist was my pal, Henny. Hand on heart, I believe this was the shoot that bonded us for life.

I called the piece 'Damaged Beauty'. From the start it was a story and a half, and you'll see why.

The shoot fell on the day of the final of the 2010 football FIFA World Cup.

Janice answered the door in her underwear, which was my first sign that this wasn't going to be an ordinary day.

The doorstep was much lower than the front door, so I basically said hello to her crotch.

I could see she was emotional and almost immediately she gave me a big hug that went on far too long for total strangers. She would not let go. She was crying. I remember trying to stay calm, all the while thinking: "What the hell is going on here?"

It transpired that her dog, Lloyd, had been attacked in the dog park that morning, had sustained serious injuries, and was currently in surgery. That would do it for anyone not just Janice.

Here's the intro for the story:

Janice Dickinson has not had a good morning. She's in tears when the Closer team arrive at her gorgeous home in Bel-Air for our 'naked' photo shoot and is waiting to hear from her vet.

Turns out, that after her daily morning yoga session, she'd taken her beloved dogs Lloyd, an English bulldog, and Chester, an English Labrador, to the park where Lloyd was then viciously attacked by a red setter.

Sitting in the make-up chair wearing teeny-tiny shorts and a black sports bra, she has tears streaming down her face and her mobile phone clutched between her hands.

*This is not the Janice Dickinson we're used to seeing on television. Famous for her mouthy, who-gives-a-f*** attitude, she might be feeling fragile, but she firmly refuses our offer to postpone the shoot.*

"I will do my very best but if you see a sad face you'll know why," she says firmly, while directing her make-up artist Pauline to do something about the 'cargo ship bags' under her eyes. "You will see a 55-year-old who takes good care of herself and I want your readers to know that today I am one sad bitch but I don't cancel. I will never cancel. You want to talk body image, let's do it. I want the English to know that they're still getting their Janice."

We sat in her kitchen as she was having her hair and make-up done. I took my tape recorder out as I tried to set the ball rolling with the interview. My thinking was that if I start early, I might actually get it in the bag before the footie ends.

Fat chance.

She shouted a lot of things at me in between the tears.

Literally, she would yell at my face.

From my transcript I can see that Janice's rapid-fire conversation went something like this:

"SIT UP STRAIGHT!"

"ARE YOU HUNGRY?"

"WHERE ARE THE FUCKING QUESTIONS?"

"I LOVE THE FUCKING BRITISH!"

There was no way I would be able to sail on in the usual manner and ask, "So Janice, what you do in your spare time?," and expect a calm response.

Roll with the punches.

I thought she seemed hyper-active. She was definitely vocal. During her floods of tears there were many worried looks exchanged between me, Simon, and Henny and also Janice's assistant, who was doing his best to attend to her needs.

As we began our chat she turned to me and asked, "Do you want a beer?"

It wasn't so much a question, more a statement. She walked to the fridge and retrieved two ice-cold bottles.

Everyone in the room declined, I said yes.

I'd driven to the shoot and wouldn't normally drink on a job but here's why I took that beer.

I knew I had to gain her trust and this was one way of doing that.

I could already see that it was going to be a long day. And also, more importantly, she wasn't going to take no for an answer.

There's no way I'm going to repeat half of what she said and nothing incendiary made the interview. But let me tell you this, Janice can tell a story. She also used the c-word more times than I have ever heard on a shoot.

Afterwards I wrote this to my commissioning editor: *It's not often you get to meet someone who is so totally uncensored. It made a real change I can tell you.*

Through the tears and the beers, she also took her vitamins. I've never seen a woman with more supplements. It was a veritable wall of pills and while it seemed odd to me then, now I'm older I have followed in her footsteps. I may not have a wall but I do tend to rattle.

Putting all that aside, she was absolutely incredible in front of the camera.

That woman knows how to turn it on. It was a 'naked' shoot so we saw every inch of her – and I mean *every* inch – but she was utterly empowered and magnificently uninhibited. She was mesmerising to watch, taking direction and contorting herself into the most incredible and beautiful lines.

Naturally, the photos were finished long before the interview was in the bag and so unsurprisingly, I found myself home alone with Janice after everyone else had left.

Janice and I sat in her garden with another beer but not before she'd insisted that I tour her house.

At this stage, I just let her lead because there was no way I was going to be able to rein in Janice Dickinson. By then, I don't really think I wanted to.

She was sad because her daughter was away at camp. She wanted me to see inside Savannah's bedroom and I said no because I felt it was an invasion of her daughter's privacy. Janice wasn't having any of it.

We sat on Savannah's bed and Janice cried some more about missing her. I gave her another hug.

She said this about how the public perceived her: "*They all say nasty things about me. Everyone has an opinion. I let you in on how crazy I want you to think I am but you've seen my home and how I live as a mom and I'm the most normal protective mom on the planet. My children don't lie to me, they're not homophobic, and I'm really proud of them.*"

As we walked around the house, I commented off-the-cuff: "*You're a damaged beauty.*"

She loved it. "*That's genius. I am a damaged beauty. Look, I'm going through the menopause and it's hell. I'm on hormone replacement and I get sweats. When you leave here after the shoot, I'll feel like something the cat dragged in. What you see on TV, forget about it; it's an act but if I'm not crazy Janice on TV people will change channels.*"

She found a Post-It note and scribbled the words 'Damaged Beauty' on it and put it on her fridge saying, "*That can be the name of my next book.*"

We sat in the garden and finished the interview. At this point I really wanted to leave but could see that she wanted me to stay and hang out, so I thought, what the hell, let's sit and shoot the breeze for a bit.

She asked me about my film-making and so I told her I'd written a script that had won a film competition. She immediately picked up her phone and called her ex-husband, Simon Fields, who is a movie producer (*Funny Bones*, *Serendipity,* and *Shall We Dance?*). Bless him, he actually answered the call which made me feel slightly uncomfortable.

She insisted I talk to him about my movie. After thrusting her phone into my hand, what ensued was an awkward conversation with a man I didn't know.

He was polite, and I got the feeling that it wasn't the first time this kind of thing had happened. It was slightly bonkers of Janice but also very LA and very sweet.

We talked a little longer and then I made my excuses and left.

It was evening by now and I was exhausted from trying to handle the situation and also from trying to chase answers to questions.

She wouldn't answer anything about body size or weight. I only stress that because I know that commissioning editors and magazines have a style and expect certain boxes to be ticked. I ticked barely any of the boxes with Janice. Somehow though, it worked out even better than if she had. As I said, she was a breath of fresh air.

Roll with the punches.

A reply to a question that would normally be straight forward elicited this response (from my transcript):

"Dress, weight, heights, it doesn't fucking matter everybody out there. I'm not the type to live up to. Look in the mirror, take a good look at yourself and figure out your type and

then stand under a naked light in the day.

Do I want to look better in the arse or the armpits? Either way it's going to flab out with or without children. Do you want a yoga body, a runner's body, or do you want to look good in a pair of jeans? We're too obsessed. No.

All women are self-obsessed, look at the queens of England squeezing into corsets. I love queens because without them I would never had made it New York, they recognised in me our power to be fabulous."

I loved her answers. She was interesting and she was honest. She walked to the beat of her own drum. It was my job that day to fall in with her rhythm if only for a few hours.

But it was tough too. The day took so many twists and turns, not least because it was so unpredictable. Janice, however, delivered in front of the camera. It was just the bit around all that which required some experienced navigation.

I called her assistant the next day to say thanks for the interview and follow-up on the dog's progress. I'm happy to say that Lloyd made a full recovery.

I like to think that Janice enjoyed her day with me and the team but more importantly I think that through the tears she also managed to convey a wonderful message of strength.

Yes, I honestly do.

She said this, which I love, "*Constantly focusing on the external makes you look inside more but I see beauty in everything. You can do anything you want, it's just how you see yourself. Look, I'm 55, I've got two kids, been on magazine covers, have great friends, and two dogs, but I still haven't figured it out. All of us, we're just on one long journey.*"

Agree. We are all just on one long journey and rolling with the punches is part of that. Figure it out as you go along. It's an adventure and one you should relish.

As Larry King told me over a salty hollowed-out bagel of his job as a talk show host and journalist: "*I never lost that kid-in-a-candy-store feeling*".

Be like Larry and you won't go far wrong.

HEADLINES:

Be adaptable and open to the experience.
Roll with the punches as they will come thick and fast.
Use your instinct to react in a way that will help your story.
Go with the flow but don't lose sight of your goal.
Enjoy the crazy. You may even learn from it.

CHAPTER 11

WORKING AGAINST A TICKING CLOCK

We're around the halfway mark and the clock is indeed ticking.

If this was an interview by now, I'd be well and truly settled into the rhythm of the chat, scanning my questions to make sure I was hitting all my story beats and making mental notes to cover new ground or go back over anything that may have piqued my interest.

If you've got a good memory, then you'll recall this book started with me talking about how often I've been asked if I've ever interviewed Ryan Gosling.

The good news is that the answer to this sweet mystery will be revealed later in this book.

The bad news is that we're not quite there yet.

I thought it might be fun to have a breather from the nuts and bolts of interviewing celebrities to tell you about some of the utterly random encounters I had in Los Angeles with the super famous.

None of these anecdotes involve Ryan but one of the joys of living in or around Hollywood is that you get to see exceptionally famous people out and about doing normal non-starry things and living their normal lives.

Going over thousands of emails in my inbox for this book I came across this long-forgotten missive, written to a pal in February 2011.

I wrote:

My friend trains at Equinox Spa and Gym in West Hollywood. She said that Puff Daddy (Sean Combs) has been in there this week training with a personal trainer. (Getting in shape for the Oscar parties this weekend?) But that he keeps taking lots of breaks to go to the water fountain so that (in her opinion) he can check out the chicks.

In 2009 I'd arranged to meet a friend at a Starbucks in Studio City. I was early so I ordered a coffee and found a table where I could work on my laptop. At the table next to me I realised that a relatively young guy was being interviewed by a similarly young girl. I was shamelessly earwigging and it seemed to me that the interview wasn't flowing particularly well. It wasn't awful by any means but to me she seemed nervous.

After she left, I leaned over, told him I was a journalist and asked him who he was and what he was being interviewed for. Turns out it was for a student mag; his name was Adam Devine and he'd just moved to Hollywood.

He explained that he was a comedian and his pilot had been green lit to series that very day by Comedy Central. He was naturally thrilled.

I have since watched his career go stratospheric with some kind of weird, misplaced maternal pride. His show, *Workaholics*, ran for six years and he went on to become a big star appearing in *Modern Family* and also the *Pitch Perfect* movies.

In 2012 I attended a friend's birthday party at the Roosevelt Hotel, on Hollywood Boulevard. The hotel is a gorgeous landmark with lots of interesting nooks and crannies and is famous in so many ways. It was named after the 26th president of the United States, Theodore Roosevelt, and the first Academy Awards were held there in 1929.

It was also where Marilyn Monroe lived for a couple of years, and where she posed for her first commercial photographic shoot by their pool, which now features a mural courtesy of David Hockney.

On this occasion my friend had rented the rather swanky bowling alley they have stowed away in the hotel. As we were playing, a young woman asked if she could share my sofa. I looked up and saw it was star of early reality hit *The Simple Life* and Hollywood mom, Nicole Richie, who was out with a friend.

Leaving that evening myself and a friend made our way to the valet area at the back of the hotel. We hadn't been there long when a people carrier came to a halt in front of us. A security guard quickly asked us to move. We didn't because weren't really in the way. He impressed upon us that they had VIPs coming through and needed to clear the area.

I told him that they were totally safe with me. He looked at me sideways, figured out quickly that I wasn't a threat, and left us alone. Moments later, six feet in front of us, Whitney Houston's late daughter Bobbi Kristina, her then boyfriend Nick Gordon and Whitney's mother Cissy Houston got out of the car. It was only a short time after Whitney had passed away and I felt a pang of sadness.

In Hollywood you're always aware that the stories the world is watching are constantly unfolding in front of you.

It's not always the celebrities currently in the headlines that can thrill. At a friend's house the actor Richard

Chamberlain – he of *Dr Kildare* and *The Thorn Birds* fame – poured me tea from a teapot. He was a star from a different era and I was thrilled to meet him. Still a gentleman, still handsome, I admit that particular encounter made me feel a little giddy.

In a storyline that could have been lifted directly from *Curb Your Enthusiasm* I accidentally spilled a vodka and cranberry down Larry David's leg one night in a bar. It was most unfortunate but the characteristic withering look he gave me was totally worth it.

I've been to a lot of movie screenings, and you get especially spoiled in Hollywood because many times at the end of the movie, the cast, and director will appear for a question-and-answer session. This isn't always for the press, it's what the producers do to ensure that as many industry people as possible see the film, so they'll set up screenings for organisations such as BAFTA, AMPAS, the DGA, PGA, and SAG, etc. Even now I sit for longer than I should in a cinema watching the credits roll, waiting for an A-lister to amble out and explain how they found their emotional nexus.

One balmy night I was invited to an early screening of Sandra Bullock's movie *The Blind Side* at the ArcLight theatre in Hollywood. I always liked the ArcLight because they have actual costumes from the movies they're showing on display in the lobby. Just another perk of the location. The costumes are always minuscule, and I now realise that sadly in this lifetime I have at least 40% more body mass than required to be a film star.

As I made my way from the car park to the foyer, I walked past a short red carpet that had been set up in front of the cinema's entrance. It was maybe 30 feet long if that. There was a rope and a small backdrop emblazoned with logos and maybe half a dozen people milling around, including a couple of photographers.

The set up was so quiet I almost didn't look over at who was being photographed but I did (I wasn't called 'nose ointment' by my dad for nothing).

On the red carpet were Angelina Jolie and Brad Pitt. Yes, those two.

I stood there for a moment, trying to wrap my head around what I was seeing. They were stunning; other-worldly, polished, angular, and well, just over there.

No one else seemed that bothered. It was almost as if this red-carpet moment wasn't happening, or that it was just happening for me. Angelina's brother, James Haven, also stepped in to have his photograph taken. He was similarly angular and other-worldly looking.

Later, I discovered that this quiet photo call was ahead of a screening of Angelina's directorial debut, *In the Land of Blood and Honey*.

As I scooted into the cinema, a woman held the door open for me. Such manners! Step forward, Gwen Stefani. Good grief, I thought: "What is going on here tonight?"

Naturally, at the end of *The Blind Side* screening, Sandra Bullock walked out on stage and by that time I was thinking to myself that I doubt I'll ever experience such a low-key, star-studded evening again (so far, no).

But where does this leave us in terms of this book?

The title of this chapter is called 'Working Against A Ticking Clock' but what have you learnt about that while I've been regaling you with my tales of memorable celebrity encounters?

Move in closer and I'll tell you.

Time is running out. The chapter is almost at an end and I haven't even really started to get to the point.

That's the lesson.

When you interview a celebrity, you will never have enough time.

Never.

Tangents will be explored, tributaries will open up, and stories will be told but ultimately you will be sitting there towards the end of your time panicking about getting everything you need. And you will most likely be kicking yourself for listening to that smoke and mirrors anecdote which was no doubt charming but absolutely no use to you or your editor.

Somehow, given all the distractions which include being in the presence of the very charming human being sitting in front of you, you need to keep an eye on the time.

It's easy to become distracted, especially when whoever you're talking to drifts off into anecdote territory.

Jeff Goldblum, who I met at the *Jurassic World* junket in London, is a gorgeous man with the best stories. He likes to tell them at length, and he loves to use the English language. Sitting in front of him listening to him talk is akin to being hypnotised. John Malkovich was also similar in terms of hypnotic verbiage.

And that's lovely if you're at a dinner party but not so relaxing when cameras are turning on a sound stage, there's only limited time to get through all the questions and time is quite literally money.

While you're doing your job you must be mindful of where you are in the interview, where you need to go, and why you should dedicate part of your brain to timekeeping.

If necessary, turn to the publicists or producer in the room and ask how much time you have left. Once you know that, you can mentally calculate what you still have to get through, what can be ditched, and what you absolutely must cover before you're shown the door.

If I know that time is going to be tight I'll look at my questions, which are in sections, and then make sure I ask the first two which I'll have placed there knowing they're the most important. I will then try to ask those two questions so that I know I've covered every area, even if it's thin on the ground in terms of detail.

Confusingly, I'm now going to say that sometimes you should do exactly the opposite if what you're getting in terms of detail is gold. You will know when you're hearing something that's going to get everyone excited. Use your judgement and keep going down that track. But if it's just entertaining waffle, be ruthless and shut it down.

"Okay, that's great, let's move on," will usually do the trick.

Occasionally you will be gifted a couple more minutes by a generous publicist but once you hear the words "Five minutes" or "Can you make this your last question", your mind will be whirring at a thousand miles an hour.

You will be screaming inwardly: “HAVE I GOT EVERYTHING I NEED?”

The answer will always be “No” and you will have a split second to ask your final one or two questions. Hopefully, at this stage your gut will tell you what those are.

As we explored earlier, sometimes it only takes 30 seconds to get a good answer to a question and, funnily enough, knowing that an interview is about to wrap up means you may get more of a headline-worthy answer than you were expecting.

People tend to speed up at the end of interviews and will maybe throw something out there in an act of relieved hubris.

I remember interviewing the Olympic diver Tom Daley in December 2016 ahead of his recipe book launch, which was all about healthy, organic, home-cooked food (the type of food that will sustain you through the Olympics and beyond).

I didn’t have a lot of time and found myself racing to get through everything but when one of his PR team uttered the dreaded words “Final question” I knew there was only one question I could ask and no waffle.

I had to pick wisely so I opted for an emotional heart-string puller about Tom’s late father Robert, who had never met Tom's then fiancé (now husband), the Oscar winning script-writer Dustin Lance Black.

I asked, "*What would your dad have made of Dustin*?"

From my transcript, Tom replied, "*I think they would have got on a treat I really do. It's quite funny because my dad was always a joker and 90% of what came out of his mouth wasn't serious. Any situation. So, I think they would have got on really well.*"

The headline that ran with the article was 'I wish my dad could have met Lance'. That last question was asked in a split second and it hit the bullseye.

I also remember Tom's own clock was ticking loudly because he actually sprinted out of the building, which was near London Bridge, to get to his diving practice. I've never been in the presence of such a fizzy, glowing energy. I felt revitalised merely looking at him. Olympians really do possess unfathomable fitness.

I like to end an interview on an emotional high if appropriate or doable. I think in terms of a profile piece it leaves the reader with a lot more to think about than "What was the last box set you binged?" (which is a question that sometimes has merit just not as a zinger to the heart).

Some last gasp HURRY UP THE CLOCK IS TICKING questions I've asked in previous interviews that have proved to be revealing are:

To Ryan Phillippe (the other other Ryan) in October 2011
Are you frugal?

"I'm not frugal – don't spend a lot of time thinking about money and you can't take it with you and you put up with so much junk sometimes so it's okay to reward yourself. I'm not frivolous. No sports cars or $100,000 sports cars. I'm simpler than that. Definitely."

To Lisa Kudrow in October 2008:
Do you allow your son to watch your work?

"The first thing that Julian saw was Friends, *but not because he put it on but his older cousin put the DVD on and he said: 'Mum is in that.' His reaction was good.*

*Some of my movies are really dark – he'll discover him on his own. He knows I work, I did this [*Hotel for Dogs*] so he could see it because I've turned down certain guest spots on kids' shows because I know he would like it but I have to draw the line. It can't all be for him."*

To Gerard Butler in June 2009
What does that bracelet that you're wearing signify?

"It's from India. There's a blessing that you do. On the banks of the Ganges, they cremate all the bodies, wash, pray, and drink the water and we swam in there. It was an amazing experience, came out of there high as a kite. I had a two-hour blessing thing where they throw yoghurt all over the place."

Just because it's the last question doesn't mean it has less worth. Make the most of every second.

The ticking clock is also useful in terms of adrenaline. Yes, you will have plenty of it coursing through your veins already but hey, why not add one more element into the mix?

If time is tight, I set my iPhone in front of me with the timer running. That way I can glance down and see exactly where we are – and then if the publicist or manager tries to short-change me, I can argue my case. "But you said 20 minutes and it's only been 17 which means I still have three to go."

Wave your phone in the air while you do this. It's obnoxious but a well-placed dramatic gesture can work, especially in the presence of thespians.

This is also a good time to ask a tricky question. If they're going to throw you out of the room, you might as well take a punt on asking it while you're already leaving.

And if you feel as if your time has been thin on the ground, don't switch off your tape recorder. Keep it running and throw out questions as you pack up. Smile and thank everyone profusely as you leave the room because they'll totally know what you're playing at.

Head to hospitality and collapse in a heap. Check your devices just in case they haven't recorded and breathe a huge sigh of relief when you realise they have. Jot down your colour notes while you drink a large coffee.

And finally, treat yourself to a giant pastry from the spread available because it's not just Tom Daley who needs to keep his strength up.

HEADLINES:

Always be aware of the time, and how much you have left.
Rein in a celebrity who is talking too much (unless it's the anecdote of the century).
Section your questions to make prioritising them easier in the moment.
Ditch the predictable, filler questions.
Follow your instinct when asked for your last question and go for it.

CHAPTER 12

PRESS CONFERENCE ETIQUETTE

In simple terms, a press conference is the art of putting a person or group of people in front of a room full of journalists, with the intention of making some kind of announcement. Generally, once the announcement has been made, the floor is open to questions from the collective media.

Americans call them 'pressers' which seems to be catching on in the UK but I will never use the word 'presser' because that's not what I call them and it doesn't take a lot more effort to say the words 'press conference'. Presser also sounds like a character from one of Danny Boyle's early movies.

You'd think it would be comforting to get lost in a crowd but I've never really enjoyed press conferences.

They're effective in that if there is only limited time with the talent everyone gets a nibble.

But they're also utterly intimidating and generally useless in terms of landing an exclusive. The reality is that you will never get anything different from anyone else unless you have a serendipitous Anthony Edwards moment. But remember, that happened to me just once in 30 years.

I find them unbelievably stressful because you never know if you're going to be able to ask a question and what will happen if you do.

On a positive note, so few people tend to put their hands up that I can't remember time running out before everyone who wants to has had a chance to ask their question. I'm talking movie or TV press conferences not news related press conferences which are another story entirely.

Before the talent is presented you will be shown into the room to take your seat. Sometimes footage of the movie, the full movie, or an episode or two is screened. After that, once the talent are seated there'll be a moment of frenzied activity while the assembled journalists set their recorders to record and place them in front of said talent.

Sometimes if you're near enough, say for instance you're seated in the front row, you may hold on to your device but many times there is a scrum for 'pole position' on the table.

You will then go back to your seat utterly convinced that your tape recorder or recording app is not working and spend most of your time trying to see if you can see the red light on/volume levels or timer moving.

Occasionally, a famous person seated at the table will touch your recording device and this will set your heart racing but not in a good way. You will most probably imagine they have switched it off somehow but be too mortified to get up in front of a crowd and check it.

Back in the day when people used tape cassettes you might hear one click to the off position and then your heart would stop again. If the talent were nice, they would hold it up and say, "Someone's recorder just stopped." Then that journalist would have to leap up from their anonymous chair and rush to turn the tape over or exchange it for another. Meanwhile, the press conference would fall silent while everyone watched said hack as they fumbled with their machine. I tell you, the ending to *Speed* is less stressful.

After the screening, if there is one, there's an introduction to the talent from whoever is leading the panel. They walk on to polite applause. The moderator may ask them some prepared questions to get everyone comfortable. Usually there are a few laughs, unless it's *Schindler's List* or something equally weighty. Then the person leading the panel throws it open to the floor.

At this point a few brave souls – possibly including you – will stick their hands in the air. Once you're chosen, you get to speak. Sometimes you may be required to use a microphone which you have to wait for as it makes its way slowly over to you, usually from some opposite corner of the room. Eventually you're handed a mic. It's rather like drunken office karaoke but devoid of any element of fun.

The mic is passed to you by a publicist or their assistant in order for you to spit out your question at an embarrassing volume. It sounds loud enough to you, yet you'll probably have to repeat it because you will be a stuttering tongue-tied mess. At other times you just have to shout and hope for the best.

Before you ask your question, you will need to state your name and the outlet you're there to represent. Sounds simple but even that becomes a mangled tongue-twister given that a panel of A-list talent and a sea of jaded journalists will be staring at you, or worse, totally ignoring you. You will probably forget your name and the reason you were born.

Really, it's just a hugely stressful form of public speaking without the wedding disco and a chance to cop off with the best man afterwards.

Just the thought of a press conference makes my stomach turn, even when I'm wearing my journalist hat. The journalist's hat by the way should always be in your toolbox. Wearing it means you can turn up anywhere and nose around asking all manner of questions but in this instance you'll also need a tin helmet, a giant pair of balls and skin so thick that even elephants stop to admire your hide.

Please, if you're a journalist and you actually like covering celebrity junket press conferences get in touch and tell me why. I just can't fathom why anyone would enjoy these things.

Now, I realise this miserable summation is probably not helping you in any way but stay with me, we'll get there. I've been doing this for a long time, but no one said it was going to be easy and doing it over and over doesn't necessarily help. In all honesty, when it comes to press conferences the more I do the more allergic I get.

The trick here I feel is to avoid making yourself look like an utter fool in front of a room full of your contemporaries, while at the same time getting a quote that might actually make it into the copy.

I'm sweating just thinking about it because it's almost impossible.

And just for the record I've never seen a press conference go the way it does in *Notting Hill* when Hugh Grant bursts into the ballroom at The Ritz London and immediately gets to ask all the questions – including a pseudo marriage proposal – to Julia Roberts without anyone else batting an eyelid. That's the movies so we'll let that one go but just so you know, what he does is a big nope in real life.

I think – no, I know – that my fear of press conferences goes back to the time I was sent by that now defunct TV listings mag to a *Cracker* press conference.

The TV series *Cracker*, starring our favourite Hagrid Robbie Coltrane, was huge at the time so there was great excitement about the fact it was returning to the small screen for what I think was its third series.

This was before email so I have no note of the exact date or location but it was in the mid-nineties, at a London hotel and at the height of *Cracker-mania* (can't remember if it was called that but it worked for the Osmonds so let's go with it).

As I was leaving the office, my editor asked me specifically to ask Mr Coltrane what it was like being a sex symbol.

"Leave it with me, boss lady!" I probably didn't say (but no doubt nodded and gave off the impression that it would be a breeze).

I remember leaving the office in a slump; it seems instead of sitting in anonymously in the crowd I would have to ask an actual question. In front of actual people. And not just to anyone but to Robbie Coltrane who was an imposing chap on a small screen, so what the hell would he be like in real life?

I was dreading it already. In fact, I'm dreading it again as I'm writing this, and it was over 20 years ago.

Let's backtrack for a second.

Robbie Coltrane is a brilliant comedic and dramatic actor, but he is not, in my opinion, what you would call traditionally movie star handsome. However, at this particular time in his career and television history, he'd gained a big following because of the show, which was created by the genius writer Jimmy McGovern.

Mr Coltrane played Dr Edward 'Fitz' Fitzgerald, an alcoholic, foul-mouthed, cynical, anti-hero, criminal psychologist. These really are all the most awful traits in a man, so naturally 'Fitz' became an instant heartthrob to women everywhere.

I arrived at the hotel and soon enough we were ushered into the room where the presser – no, that's still not working for me – where the press conference was about to start.

There were rows of chairs, but I decided to sit front and centre.

WHAT? I hear you cry. Why would I do that?

Well, I always try to sit front and centre. This is not just bravado but when I don't feel I can do anything that well, I always put myself at the front, therefore giving myself no way to escape. I do the same at my Pilates class. I have a bad back and can only ever do around 40% of the exercises but I always place my mat front and centre in order to brave it out. There's nowhere to hide and I feel that just being in the room means I will ultimately give it my best, even if my best is not as good as the bendy miracle lady contorting herself on the mat next to me.

The same goes for press conferences. Front and centre.

The bonus of this insanity is that, for example, you get to sit right in front of Jennifer Aniston at the *Horrible Bosses* press conference in New York, and she smiles at you and you believe for a brief moment in your life that you could actually be her BFF.

Given that at the *Horrible Bosses* press conference I only had one page to fill for the Aussie *Telegraph* and no chance of a one-to-one interview with Jen, the piece came out great. Remember all that stuff earlier about colour? Well, here's the intro and it's like we were BFFs:

You'd think that the weight of all that's been written about actress Jennifer Aniston would leave her bent double and dragging enough baggage to fill a 747.

But what you think and what you get are two completely different things.

Today, she's at the Waldorf Astoria New York, one of the oldest hotels in New York, and the epitome of faded grandeur. The legendary landmark (the building, not Aniston), takes up an entire block just south of Central Park, and is known for its famous Waldorf salad and close-up magic shows.

So, it's fitting that Aniston, who is one of the most talked about and photographed women on the planet, appears out of nowhere like a designer-clad conjuror's assistant.

It's impossible not to be drawn to her energy. Her smile is genuine, her luscious blonde hair bobs gently like driftwood on a lake, and her eyes are wide and expansive.

Strikingly, she looks as if she has been dipped in honey. But not just any honey; the most expensive, delicious, golden honey in the world. If she could bottle that incredible skin colour, it would undoubtedly be as popular as 'the Rachel', the hairstyle she made famous on Friends, *and that she recently confessed to hating.*

She's wearing soft grey tones that complement her syrupy hue; a grey Tom Ford skirt, a Calvin Klein bustier, and Michael Kors shoes. And all the while, her chunky gold watch glints in the sunlight that's streaming through the giant windows, which have been dressed in heavy Louis XIV drapes.

For a woman who appears to be forever tied to her superstar ex-husband, his equally famous wife, and their rainbow brood (if you don't know who they are, you probably only speak Klingon), she's supremely confident in herself. But it wasn't always that way.

"I'm happier with myself now," says the 42-year-old, before joking, "At the age of 60, I think I'm doing pretty good."

She laughs, then adds, "I was just so uncomfortable with myself in my twenties, but I'm absolutely more comfortable in my body as I've gotten older."

Does she think that older women, who are sexy and confident, are scary to men? She exclaims, "I think men are intimidated by women of any age!"

I didn't ask any questions at that press conference, so those quotes exist purely because someone else was brave/stupid enough to speak words out loud.

And while those were the same quotes that the world and his wife had, at least I managed to put a little personal spin on things.

Although – breathes deeply – if I ever get to interview Jennifer in person I promise to a) not lick her skin to find out if it really is made out of honey, and b) not to bring up Brad Pitt in the intro. Time to move on now, people!

So that was July 2011 but let's rewind a good 15 years or so from there and continue to revel in the details of my unfinest hour with the cast of *Cracker*.

The press conference started and after a while I seized my moment and stuck my hand in the air. I was awarded the floor and asked Mr Coltrane the Pulitzer prize-winning question: "What does it feel like to be a sex symbol?"

It's fair to say, and this a magnificent understatement, that he wasn't impressed with this line of enquiry in any way, shape, or form.

Visibly and vocally irritated, he said something along the lines of: "*What a stupid question. I'm not answering that.*" And then as I recall, he proceeded to indulge in an impassioned rant about the idiotic press and how ridiculous we were and oh, you know what, I've blocked most of it out. Suffice to say, he was really pissed off. And all his ire was directed at little ole me.

I went bright red, overheated, and squirmed in my chair. It was my worst nightmare. I had to sit it out as a room full of journos, publicists, and *Cracker* talent looked at me, either feeling my pain or laughing at it. I don't exactly know BECAUSE I WAS DYING INSIDE.

It was belittling and even now, all this time on, I still fail to see what the problem was. I certainly didn't appreciate being made to feel that way when I was merely doing my job. And Mr Coltrane, who was in the room and seated on the panel at the *Cracker* press conference – the show he was the star of – must surely have expected that he would be asked questions he liked and some questions that he didn't. Obviously, the whole sex symbol thing was anathema to him. Fair enough. But while it wasn't a great question, it wasn't the worst either.

I said nothing back. If the same thing was to happen to me now, at this stage of my career, I'd most definitely fight my corner in some way but in the mid-nineties I was young and well, young.

The horror of that moment has stayed with me. I remember afterwards talking to my fellow journos and them being extremely supportive. It was a light-hearted question and not meant to offend. They understood and I appreciated their support but ultimately it didn't make me feel any better. It's never nice being hauled over the coals by anyone, and especially someone who you've admired for a long time. I told the story with dramatic relish back at the office – got a few ahhs and a few laughs – and wrote up what I had.

It took years for me to have the courage to raise my hand again and when I did, I dropped another clanger.

Yes, another one. I'm sharing this so you can avoid this hideous rite of passage and skip straight to silent. From now on, nobody should ask questions at press conferences.

Let's all make a pact now to keep our mouths shut!

This time it was at the *Hugo* press conference in New York, in November 2011.

The print press conference featured Chloë Grace Moretz, Asa Butterfield, Emily Mortimer, co-producers Graham King, and John Logan, and Brian Selznick the author of the Hugo Cabret novel. Oh, and Sir Ben Kingsley. Just soak that up for a minute. Gandhi.

Hugo, a charming movie, was directed by Martin Scorsese and eventually became a huge hit winning four Oscars including Best Cinematography.

This idiot here (that's me) decided they just had to raise their hand and ask Sir Ben a question. I was sitting middle and centre. The front had filled out too fast.

And so, the question I asked was…here we go, I'm already dying inside a little, it was so stupid. The question was: "What was it like working with Martin Scorsese for the first time?"

To which an entire room full of people turned around and almost in unison said, "They worked together on *Shutter Island*!"

Which had come out the year before.

Remember, when I wrote that really, really long chapter on doing your research?

Well, this is why you do your research.

I have no excuse. I don't know how I missed it. Hands up. Fair cop, guv. It was a massive error but Sir Ben, charm personified, answered my question in full, and talked at length about working with 'Marty'. Thank you, Sir Ben. I did not feel belittled by Sir Ben, but I was annoyed with myself.

I was at the junket to interview Chloë Grace Moretz so ultimately, I didn't have to ask anything at the press conference, I just wanted to get involved. Why? I do not know.

Since *Hugo* I don't think I've asked one question at a press conference although I've been to many more. I am now the Trappist monk of pressers (no, still no).

Asking around for nuggets of wisdom to impart within this chapter the overriding advice from my journalist friends was: "Stay silent and let everyone else talk."

It seems I'm not the only one who finds them difficult.

I suppose the vow of silence is okay up to a point but there are times when you absolutely must ask a question and you will have to get on with the job at hand.

I do get the feeling though that most people outside of the business think journalists saunter into a press conference full of attitude desperate for a shouting match but that couldn't be further from the truth. The testament to that is that the back rows always fill up quickly.

Side note: *most journalists dislike facing the press themselves. It's one thing asking the questions and sitting on the other side of the camera but quite the shock to the system when the tables are turned.*

When I was a cub reporter on *The Echo*, I was dispatched to Downing Street to pick up the Queen's Birthday Honours list. Remember, this was decades before email and to ensure we had the list in our sweaty palms and could beat the competition by publishing the results seconds after embargo I was sent to bring this sensitive information back to the office.

Fun fact: *that same year, my favourite Miss Marple Joan Hickson was made an OBE, as was actor Michael Crawford, and Anthony Hopkins became a CBE.*

It was also the day after Margaret Thatcher had won her third election and the world's press were assembled outside Number 10. The wall of cameras was terrifying. They were trained on me as I approached the famous black door with its shiny gold Number 10.

At this stage Thatcher hadn't appeared in front of the press for her post-win photo call so the atmosphere was fully charged.

The wall of media seemed skyscraper high and my knees literally quaked as I was ushered inside the house. Once inside I was instructed to wait in the lobby. I had a letter on me which identified me as a representative of *The Echo*. That was taken away and I stood there in silence trying to process where I was standing just one month out of journalism school.

I listened and yes, from a room in front of me, I could hear the Prime Minister talking to television journalist Sir Robin Day, who was about to conduct his post-election interview. It was utterly surreal.

Out of a side door an assistant appeared with a fat manila envelope that was marked for the *Basildon & Southend Evening Echo* and I was shown the door.

Remember, the world's press were on the other side and expecting the PM to appear. As the door opened, I could already hear the sound of the cameras clicking frenetically. My heart was racing.

Then I walked out, me, baby-faced Lisa Marks, aged 18 and 11 months from Southend-on-Sea, not our record-breaking Prime Minister gloating in her third successive election win.

I was instantly blinded by the flashes and the noise of the cameras which seemed to shatter my ear drums. As I scuttled away towards the street the noise quickly died down and I heard someone mumble, “She’s no one.”

Very true, that man, very true.

It was horrible. Groups of press are only a comfort zone to journalists who are used to being among them and not standing out for any reason.

However, it’s not all bad news. I remember going to the *A Knight’s Tale* print press conference in London, in 2001, which stands out for the simple reason that the late Heath Ledger was in attendance, as was his co-star Rufus Sewell. I recall that Heath was wearing a knitted beanie hat, was softly spoken, and exuded a gentle energy.

Sometimes you find yourself at the centre of a breaking story such as the time I attended the press conference for *Wall Street: Money Never Sleeps* in New York. It was September 2010 and the 45-minute press conference was held at the Ritz-Carlton Central Park. Participating talent included Michael Douglas, director Oliver Stone, Carey Mulligan, and Josh Brolin.

News had just broken that Michael Douglas, who played the reprehensible corporate raider Gordon Gekko, had throat cancer.

It was a huge story.

And there he was, for the first time in public, sitting in front of us looking slimmer than you'd expect but also healthier than you'd expect. It was revealed years later that he didn't have throat cancer but tongue cancer which he recovered from. There's no story here other than that it was interesting to see him at that time. Good for him for braving it out in front of the press.

I really enjoyed the *Mad Men* season five press conference held in Los Angeles just so I could be in the presence of a group of people who made a show I was in love with at the time. The same goes for the *Cold Feet* press conference in London in 2016. Sometimes, as a perk of the job, it's just a thrill to be part of a big TV event. I didn't ask any questions at either though.

But I will say this.

If you're attending a press conference and simply must get involved (because it's your job so you must get involved despite what I say), you should have a specific, engaging question at the ready. One that you've fact-checked within an inch of its life.

Take a deep breath, imagine the panel naked, and go for it.

Bring as much of you to the moment as you can muster. Try to block out the white noise coming from the assembled masses and focus on the job at hand.

Despite everything I've outlined above I've been to some press conferences that have paid off and been good fun. Not every question you ask at a press conference will be met with anger or opprobrium, in the same way that it won't get you a front-page story or in Hugh Grant's case, a movie star wife.

Elect to say 'I do' and not 'I don't'. You never know, you might enjoy it.

And if you do, please email and tell me why.

HEADLINES:

Don't go in the first place.

Ignore the above, it's your job! Go with the idea you will conquer.

Have a clear, concise, and interesting question ready.

Check your facts. Check them again.

Try not to let the public nature of a press conference overwhelm you.

If you get a snippy answer, don't take it personally and move on.

Don't ask anyone to marry you.

CHAPTER 13

COVERING THE RED CARPET

In the world of celebrity, walking the red carpet is seen as the ultimate symbol of success.

If you've been invited to walk one then kiddo, you've made it.

And if you've been invited to cover one, you can also give yourself a pat on the back. But before you get too smug remember it's only because somebody more senior on staff didn't want to be there because of the time they caught pneumonia waiting for the BAFTAs to start.

Kidding! It wasn't pneumonia, it was strep throat.

Your health aside, it's the talent who are most important and for them, the stakes are stratospherically high.

After all those acting classes, regional theatre tours, non-union movies, pub gigs, and stand-up routines performed to one man and a dog, plus years of dieting, spinning, and self-doubt, suddenly their ship has come in.

They're a hit and the world is watching. They're the one who has made it, a veritable media darling, a very important person – and yes, they're also probably regretting their choice of footwear as they smile-grimace for the cameras.

No matter though, they're finally important enough to be photographed by the world's press, be gifted a couture tux or gown, draped in ridiculously expensive jewellery that will almost certainly come with its own security detail, undergo some type of 'procedure' from a discreet clinic, endure a complete physical makeover and have a giant hair piece glued onto their head.

Congratulations celebrity, you are now ready to be interviewed by some extremely stressed out journalists.

Every premiere or awards show has a red carpet. They've always been useful for hyping up interest in whatever it is that's being released but in today's ravenous content-chomping world red carpets and their heavenly conveyor belt participants are, like shapewear, a perfect fit.

Serving up beautiful people on a plate, red carpets provide endless images to fill thousands of web pages in order to be judged by the less photogenic masses, as well as tasty off-the-cuff soundbites that can be transformed into click bait in mere moments.

Smiley faces all round.

This is most certainly not the place to get an in-depth celebrity interview but it can definitely be the place to capture the essence of an event, find a potential viral moment, record an embarrassing cock up, or catch a cold.

Red carpets are generally red (I know, this kind of astute observation is why you bought this book). Sometimes though, if the event's producers want to show their wacky side, they mix things up and lay down a pink, green or even a floral carpet if you're the Chelsea Flower Show and Her Majesty the Queen is in attendance. But even if they go for this kind of crazy stunt, it's still called the red carpet because 'walking the floral carpet' sounds like something you would have done in Haight-Ashbury in '69.

Out of all the red carpets in the world the most famous is the one you see every year at the Academy Awards in Los Angeles. Yes, in the world of showbiz even red carpets have their own level of celebrity.

The Oscar's red carpet is probably the most photographed bit of flooring in the world. It is surely the most anticipated. AMPAS, who are responsible for the Oscars, actually hold a photo call for the moment it's unrolled. That carpet has the kind of social media profile that most of us can only dream about.

I fell down a little red carpeted rabbit hole writing this chapter, so here are some stats from the 2018 Academy Awards:

The carpet measures 50,000 square feet.

Signature Systems Group, a flooring company from Santa Fe Springs, store and then install it. They have done this since 2008.

The carpet isn't actually red. GASP. It's more a burgundy shade designed to complement the A-listers who will walk it. The colour specification is under lock and key, rather like Colonel Sanders' fried chicken recipe.

This fluffed-up slab of (almost) red carpet is scrutinised so closely that if one thing out of the ordinary happens on it, the story can instantly make headline news or go viral.

A case in point is 'Angelina's leg', which made an appearance at the 2012 Oscars. Angelina wore a heavy velvet Atelier Versace dress with a deep slash that required her to adopt a pronounced leg stance. It was so striking that Jim Rash, who won the Best Adapted Screenplay Oscar that year for *The Descendants* and who is also a hilarious comedic actor (*Community's* Dean Pelton anyone?), felt compelled to emulate her pose when he arrived on stage to collect his statue from the actress.

During the show, the parody Twitter account @angiesrightleg was created ("You have to admit, I'm one hell of a leg"). When a Twitter account is created in real time, you know you've hit the jackpot.

Angelina was the talk of the Oscars. Not even Sacha Baron Cohen, who'd earlier thrown 'Kim Jong-il's ashes' over presenter Ryan Seacrest was able to grab as many headlines. I was even commissioned to write a story about it for *The Sunday Telegraph.*

Other notable Oscar red carpet appearances include Bjork's swan gown at the 2001 awards. Please research this dress, it's so fantastic I'm not sure why anyone else bothered to turn up during or since.

And Cher, who I once interviewed at a roundtable for the movie *Burlesque*, wore the most splendid Bob Mackie gown to the 1986 awards, where she won the Best Actress gong for *Moonstruck.*

One of my favourite red carpets was the BAFTA 2002 'soapy' red carpet in London.

Torrential rain in the capital that night caused the red carpet to turn white with soap foam. Lovely. Notable thespians such as Dame Judi Dench and Kate Winslet had their shoes ruined by the globby mess.

Stephen Fry who hosted the show said, "I think it's the years of greasy flattery given to actors which is finally bubbling up."

Many people hold Academy Awards viewing parties in LA and it's fun to watch the show in real time for a change, and not at 4 a.m. as you do in the UK. On one occasion, along with a group of likeminded reprobates, I even heckled the many feted A-listers arriving at the *Vanity Fair* party, from the Saddle Ranch Bar opposite. "Oi, J-Lo, over here!" I fear bourbon was involved but that's all you need to know about that.

Even though I reported on the culture and entertainment scene for *The Guardian* in LA, I was never asked to cover the red carpet for them or any other outlets. Some jobs will always be the domain of senior staff, but that's okay as I did many others and it's a long and gruelling day. There is a distinct lack of glitz or glamour. Just blisters and VPL. Trust me, the media professional on the ground is running on no sleep, caffeine, and nerves.

So how does it all work?

Well, before you can even step into the media pen, you need accreditation.

Back up, what's a media pen? This is the fixed point or area designated solely for the press. Media are herded together and kept 'secure' so those in charge can keep an eye on us all.

You cannot wander away from your fixed point or else chaos will follow. The royal family go on their walkabouts knowing exactly where the press will be at any given time. Journalists and photographers 'pool' their words and photographs meaning they're shared, as access is so limited. For example, at the wedding of the Duke and Duchess of Sussex in May 2018, it would have been impossible for thousands of media professionals from around the globe to attend. A few are picked and the words and images are shared.

A red carpet is similar. Access is limited. You are allocated a space behind a barrier on the red carpet and that's where you stay.

To get near a red carpet for a premiere you will need to be nominated by your outlet who must officially propose you as their representative. Once you've been approved, you'll be given details of when and where you have to be on the day of the event. It's a given that you need to look smart for your job, but the Oscars and the BAFTAs require evening attire.

You will almost certainly be told to arrive hours before the first celebrity does. Those hangry A-listers won't have even risen from their marshmallow-soft beds by the time you arrive to stand behind a metal barrier in a new outfit (that still has the label in it so you can return it later).

At the Los Angeles Film Festival in 2012 I was on hand to cover the opening night. If we ever become friendly, I'll dig out my blurry photos of Michelle Pfeiffer, Chris Pine, and Woody Allen taken on my trusty BlackBerry.

I was shown my spot behind the barrier. There was a piece of A4 paper with the words '*Lisa Marks Guardian*' written on it. I was squeezed in between a movie website and a Spanish TV station.

Saying hello to those around me I hunkered down for the long wait.

Covering a red carpet in Los Angeles during the afternoon you would think it would be warm. Nope. Freezing.

It's rarely warm covering a red carpet wherever in the world you are. I don't know what happens but I think *Death Eater Monthly* must also be invited to attend them all because the wind chill is ridiculous, even in California.

My friend, Kirsty Hatcher, covered the BAFTAs in London in 2017 when she was News Editor on *OK!* and tells me, "I've never been so cold in this country."

And she comes from Cardiff.

So my advice to you is take water (although drink it sparingly as you know the moment you step out for a pee the star of the movie will appear and you'll miss them), and snacks as you will be stuck in one spot for a long time.

Wear layers. Plenty of layers. So many layers.

Also, unless you're covering the Oscars, a trusted pair of comfortable shoes will see you right. Honestly, it's not worth the agony wearing a shoe that looks fabulous but is going to feel like you're being stabbed in the heel after twenty minutes. You will be wearing them a long, long, long time. Comfort over style every time. And look, there aren't many perks of the job but that's one. The celebrities you'll meet on the red carpet have to wear uncomfortable shoes but thankfully you don't.

One of the actors I got to interview on the LA Film Festival red carpet was Gillian Jacobs, who was walking the red carpet for Lorene Scafaria's movie *Seeking A Friend for the End of the World*, which starred Keira Knightley, Steve Carell, and Adam Brody.

Gillian, who I first became aware of for her role as uptight Britta Perry in *Community*, was doubly excited as *Community* was up for a handful of Critics' Circle Television Awards, which was happening across town at the same time. It ultimately won Best Comedy Series.

Our conversation focused on shoes. After posing for photographers, by the time she got to me she'd taken them off. I'll never forget her telling me that no matter how gorgeous every actress looks on the red carpet they're questioning their choice of footwear and probably in agony.

Obviously, I recognised Gillian but especially on movie red carpets there are plenty of people involved who you won't immediately recognise.

To ensure no one gets embarrassed when say, you're faced with the producer of *The Avengers*, a publicist will walk alongside them with a piece of paper or card telling you their name, their job, and the movie.

Side note: *I spoke to a UK journalist who has covered many red carpets in London and she swears she's never seen that done but maybe it should be*?

Covering the red carpet for the world premiere of *People Like Us* starring Chris Pine and Elizabeth Banks, I spied scriptwriter-turned-director Alex Kurtzman walking towards not just me but the world's press. I actually recognised him because I'm a film nerd and had seen him at industry panels. Rather sweetly a well-dressed lady standing next to me was trying to catch his attention.

This is what I wrote in my *LA Diary* dispatch:

Perched behind the hordes of red carpet press, Alex Kurtzman's mother-in-law stands precariously on a railing, trying to catch his attention. Looking as proud as punch, she waves emphatically in his direction, before stepping back on to the pavement. "He's talking to someone," she says with magnificent understatement. He is indeed.

I would also add that you have to be a lot more vocal at a red carpet as it's a bit of a bun fight.

Don't be shy to call out as that's what everyone else will be doing. It's not my particular comfort zone but it's necessary.

Sometimes publicists will walk down the line of press ahead of any VIP arrival to ask what it is you need and will do their best to accommodate you.

However, at a huge premiere you may not be lucky. Even if the publicist says they can get you whoever it is you want, they may not want to talk to you or your outlet, or have arrived so late they won't have time. Or, and this always seems to be the way, they'll be embroiled in some headline-making scandal the same week their movie is out and therefore instructed to talk to nobody.

There isn't much you can do about any of the above so even though it might not seem prudent, always take the time to speak to any supporting actors you get offered. I didn't get to interview Keira Knightley or Steve Carell on the red carpet that day but I spoke to Gillian and she added a nice touch of colour to my *Guardian* dispatch.

Also, and this is key, have three amazing questions prepared, and not ones that can be answered with a yes or no.

Keep the fawning to a minimum. "Oh my goodness you look totally amazing, I can't believe I'm here with you today, I so loved your new movie, what a blast, etc…" will cut into your precious seconds of access.

Count the time in seconds because it will be unusual for you to get more than 120 of them with any given celebrity. On-camera interviews might last longer but whether it's print, online, or on-camera, when the person you've been waiting for all day appears in front of you, you'd better be ready to go with your tape recorder set to record, a big smile for the camera (you must surely know by now how I feel about smiles), and a killer question.

Time is of the essence and you need to hustle. Before you know it, yours will be up and the celebrity will disappear with a wince and a hobble in a pair of kitten heels that feel as if they've been made out of razor blades.

After you add up what you've made per hour waiting outside in the elements for a soundbite or two, you will then be left wondering why you didn't take your parents' advice and become a lawyer.

Sometimes, the truth is that this job is not particularly fulfilling. Red carpets are potential pain points designed to make you feel like you've done a below par job. You probably won't have the chance to shine in your usual way. I think it's easier for on-camera journos to feel as if their presence on the red carpet has been worth it but for print journalists it can be a slog.

Saying that, it all depends on your attitude and determination. Something like the National Television Awards is a lot easier because the stars are generally more approachable, have been attending for years and know what's expected of them.

Ultimately, though, the red carpet is thrilling. The presence of the A-list, the outfits, the sound of a hundred cameras whirring and the general air of excitement is mesmerising.

I have massive respect for the women who have to walk the red carpet. It's not easy and the scrutiny they are under is immense. I know we live in a world now where we are pushed to #askhermore but actresses still have to look flawless.

Here's part of an *LA Diary* I wrote for *The Guardian* in November 2008 (please note the mention of shoes):

There's something uniquely thrilling about being in the same room as Meryl Streep.

To my mind, she's the American Dame Judi; a wonderful cake-mix of immense talent, homely mannerisms, and steely determination. I want her to make me chicken soup, take me gently by my arm, and ask me about my day.

So I felt fortunate to have pole position on the red carpet when she arrived at the opening of the AFI Festival. And I watched as the world's press went crackers.

Streep, who played a nun in the gala premiere, Doubt, *was joined on the superior floor covering by* I've Loved You So Long's *Elsa Zylberstein, Michelle Trachtenberg, her* Doubt *co-star Amy Adams (in killer Louboutins), and*

Doubt's *writer/director John Patrick Shanley, who was sporting a skinny red tie, bowling jacket, and sneakers.*

Shanley wrote Moonstruck, *meaning he's basically God. Therefore, the headline to this blog should be "God wears Converse", but that would be silly, even for me.*

To get to my coveted position behind the paparazzi-lined barriers (where I was jammed in between Real TV and Canal Plus) I had to walk the aforementioned red carpet.

Cue panic attack. The phrase "run the gauntlet" does not even come close. The carpet was springy, the lights were cornea-bustingly bright and the lenses of 100 cameras were trained on my every move as I literally sprinted past the sponsors' board.

I can now, hand-on-heart, understand why every actress on the planet under-eats, fills their face with botulism at the first sign of a feathery line and is a bag of how-do-I-look insecurities. It was, frankly, hell.

If that sounds awful then remember, at least you don't have to vacuum the damn thing.

HEADLINES:

Wear weather appropriate clothes and shoes.
Take water and snacks with you in case you're not able to leave.
Keep alert, you will only have a brief moment with the celebrity.
Write three amazing questions and be happy if you only get to ask one.
Interview supporting cast with the same enthusiasm as A-listers.

CHAPTER 14

NAVIGATING A ROUNDTABLE

These roundtables have nothing to do with *King Arthur*, not even the Hollywood remake, but there's definitely an element of going into battle when it comes to covering one.

Roundtables are similar to press conferences in that they're designed to expose talent to as many journalists as possible at once, although for me they are nowhere near as terrifying.

They can however be extremely awkward, surreal and artificial but on a good day, great fun, exhilarating, and hugely memorable. It really does depend on the mix of the people around said table and their willingness to play ball.

Like many junkets, or press-meets-the-talent scenarios, what you're required to do is weirdly counter-intuitive. Tables are used to break bread, to eat around, to drink around, to relax around. They are usually the heart of any home.

Think about how you hang out with your friends and the shorthand you have, the comfort you get from their presence, the easy laughs and emotional connections built on years of being in each other's company.

Roundtables are the opposite of this.

Your skill as a journalist here is to read the room, make judgements on when to speak or when not to speak and how best to engage the talent, all while you sit tightly packed around a table trying not to play footsie with the entertainment editor from an obscure Norwegian movie website.

At a roundtable you're essentially asking a group of strangers to share a table which is mostly *literally* round, at an upmarket hotel (so it will at least be covered in a crisp, white linen tablecloth) and instantly work together as a team.

Journalists are at heart a competitive bunch and each have their own brief to fill, so despite the fact that most publicists will ensure you're not at a roundtable with a direct competitor, everyone has their own agenda.

It's always interesting to see who you'll be in the room with. Some will be friends, and some will not. That's the simple truth. There are people who you might want to actively avoid because they talk too much or are notoriously rude, and others who you know are gracious and will add to the experience.

So as every journalist enters the suite, nods hello, and takes their seat, the energy changes. And as the chairs around the table are taken one by one it changes again and again and again.

Once everyone is seated, you wait.

After what always seems like an eternity the publicist will then throw a celebrity or two (or sometimes three) into the mix. Within milliseconds of their arrival the energy in the room changes once again.

The sands are constantly shifting and yet somehow everyone in this small space must work together to create a convivial atmosphere to get the job done.

This is a business and as I've said before, you are merely part of a giant machine.

Generally, the roundtable will run smoothly but not always and that's because people can be nervous, wary, hung-over, or bat-shit crazy.

Think of the roundtable as the starter dough, and everyone else as the added ingredients. Sometimes that bread is going to rise, other times the mix will be so off balance you'll end up with bread you could saw wood with.

For me though this is one of the joys of the job. I rather love the element of surprise, the people watching and overall adrenaline surge.

The ideal scenario is that everyone will get a chance to speak and that the conversation will be wide-ranging enough so that every journalist gets what they want within the allotted time.

Side note: *I've never seen a camera crew at a roundtable as they're generally the domain of print journalists.*

Side note two: *I've attended many roundtables but the ones with the best in-room beverages are in LA. This is important information I feel.*

But while I make roundtables sound tricky, they can also be a joy. Big stars don't often have enough one-to-one slots for smaller outlets. They will maybe do a couple of big covers in different parts of the globe to publicise a movie, so while *Vanity Fair* or *GQ* land quality time with Jennifer Lawrence or Brad Pitt, the rest of us have to take what we can.

Rarely in LA would I attend only roundtable interviews without having a one-to-one interview scheduled but one of the few times I was happy to do that was for the 2010 movie *Burlesque*, starring Cher and Christina Aguilera.

The magazine wasn't able to secure a one-to-one interview with Cher or Christina so my two interviews, which ran as separate pieces, came from the roundtables.

I didn't care, I'd sit at any shaped table to be able to share air space with Cher. It's not often you meet a bona fide legend but she's definitely up there.

The *Burlesque* junket was held at the Four Seasons Hotel Los Angeles At Beverly Hills, and the attending talent alongside Cher and Christina were Stanley Tucci, Cam Gigandet, Eric Dane, Julianne Hough, and Steve Antin. Thankfully we didn't have to speak to them all at once. That would have been one hell of a crowded roundtable and we already had 12 journos crammed into a small space (that's six too many IMHO).

The talent were paired as such: Cher & Stanley Tucci, Christina Aguilera & Cam Gigandet, Eric Dane & Julianne Hough. Steve Antin, whose sister is Robin Antin, the founder of the Pussycat Dolls, was on his own.

So that's a lot of interviews I had to sit through to get to both my ladies.

The junket confirmation email actually ends with a line written in bold type:

You are expected to participate in ALL roundtables with ALL talent.

Underneath that it says also in bold AND this time underlined:

*<u>**Please be advised that there will be no photo opportunities with any of the talent**</u>.

That's why there is no photo evidence of me standing next to Cher trying to work out how anyone's bottom can be that perfect (it was unbelievable, trust me), or many of the stars I've met in these circumstances.

The rules were worth it.

As the great woman herself might say on Twitter: **fire emoji dollar emoji heart emoji toilet bowl emoji lipstick emoji ghost emoji**.

Two things. I clearly remember Cher telling us what she'd eaten on the Sony plane the night before; three pieces of pizza, four huge ravioli, and a chocolate chip cannoli. That's a lot of hearty food. In honour of our meeting I might eat the exact same thing after finishing this chapter.

She was absolutely delightful. I remember how she described making Christina feel at ease on set. Christina had said in an earlier roundtable that she was naturally nervous meeting and working with Cher but Cher said this, "*I think she wanted to like me but she was a little nervous. I did what Meryl (Streep) did for me in Silkwood, I emailed her and said I have your back, I'm here to support you. Don't worry that I'm going to do some weird actressy shit. I'm going to help you in every way I can. I will never let you look stupid or do anything to hurt you and so we became friends*."

Legend.

Also Cher fans, she was wearing a Bob Mackie top and Jean Paul Gaultier pants that she'd had for 15 years. Bob Mackie is not just for the Oscars, he's for life!

While attending roundtables is often compulsory and can seem like a waste of time, I can tell you that it's far from that. *Sunday Magazine* always asked me to get an additional quote from either the director, the producer, or a co-star of the talent I was profiling to add perspective. From that point of view, it was important for me to be there but also, people are interesting!

Some of the people I've talked to yet never filed a word of copy from include Laurence Fishburne, Roberto Rodriguez, and Antonio Banderas.

I remember being at the *Red Riding Hood* junket at the Hyatt Regency Century Plaza Hotel, in 2011, because I was scheduled to do a one-to-one interview with Amanda Seyfried, and the director Catherine Hardwicke.

But at the roundtables I got to meet Gary Oldman. Best. Day. Ever. When he was asked by someone around the table why he'd taken the role as the movie's villain, he laughed and said it was to pay the bills. Gotta love some old-fashioned roundtable London-boy-done-good honesty.

So how do you tackle a roundtable, which is yet another pressurised, time-sensitive environment where what you get depends in part on the endeavours and attitudes of others?

The key is clear communication with your peers.

Communication. That's it.

There is a roundtable etiquette, but it all comes down to communication.

Here are some of the ground rules as I see them:

1. Say hi to everyone as they walk into the room or when you walk into the room. It immediately creates a less awkward atmosphere. I know people are grumpy nowadays, but I do this in real life and it rarely backfires.
2. Ask people where they're from and what outlets they're representing if you don't know.

3. Make small talk. You're going to be there a good long time so you may as well get to know your fellow writers.
4. Everyone is after the A-list talent, that's a given, but if you're sitting there waiting for supporting actors or the director or producers, then ask who wants what? Chances are someone will be desperate to grill Jaume Collet-Serra, Joel Silver, and Leonard Goldberg, who were the director and producers of the Liam Neeson film *Unknown*. I only needed a quote or two about January Jones, who I was interviewing later that day, so the film mag journo sitting around the table got most of the time that day.
5. When the talent walks into the room make eye contact and say hello. I can't believe how many people mumble their hellos into the tablecloth. Don't make this any more weird than it has to be.
6. Unless you've discussed it before, don't monopolise the time. Everyone is there for a reason.
7. Don't go off on a tangent. There's nothing more irritating than listening to a critique about an obscure art-house movie for no reason other than the journalist wants to show off their movie knowledge.
8. If you've asked a couple of questions step back if you

can see that others want to come in.

9. Try not to ask anything that's going to shut down the conversation.
10. Wear deodorant. These rooms can get hot and you're going to be in there a while. You're welcome.

The best example I can give of the wheels turning smoothly is the *CBS TV Junket* I attended at The Beverly Hilton in early 2011.

This really was the big one, a junket's junket.

A large ballroom is filled with tables which are then allocated to journalists from all over the world – no clashing territories – and over two or three days, a steady stream of talent is brought to each table for chats lasting up to 15 minutes.

Think of a grand ballroom scene from a period movie but replace the glasses of wine with plastic bottles of water and silverware for iPhones and recording devices. (And yes, we all sit around wearing ballgowns. Well, internally I do.)

The talent list at this particular junket was solid:

Michael C Hall – *Dexter*
Gary Sinise – *CSI: NY*
Sela Ward – *CSI: NY*
Chris Noth – *The Good Wife*
Chris O'Donnell – *NCIS: Los Angeles*
LL Cool J – *NCIS: Los Angeles*
Marg Helgenberger – *CSI: Crime Scene Investigation*
George Eads – *CSI: Crime Scene Investigation*
Tom Selleck – *Blue Bloods*
Jerry O'Connell – *The Defenders*
Jim Belushi – *The Defenders*

And from *NCIS* a raft of actors including Mark Harmon, Rocky Carroll, Shane Brennan, Cote de Pablo, Michael Weatherly, and Sean Murray.

LL Cool J!

I'd pitched a Marg Helgenberger interview to *The Scotsman's* weekend magazine and it turned out that Alison Gray, the paper's esteemed deputy editor, was a big fan of *CSI*. That's how Marg became a cover story.

Thus, with no other commissions, I found myself sitting through 18 roundtables to get my one-to-one with Marg, who told me that after leaving the show she wanted to tread the boards in London. She still hasn't – come on, Marg, the West End awaits!

I haven't owned an actual television since 2006 and I've never seen many of these shows. Hand on heart, apart from maybe Mark Harmon, I probably couldn't identify anyone from *NCIS* if my life depended on it.

We really didn't know the order we'd be seeing people, so it was potluck. But this is why roundtables are amazing. Someone delivers a really famous person to your table and then they're forced to talk to you.

It's like the worst date ever meets the best date ever.

Dexter was huge at the time so chatting to Michael C Hall was really great fun and going back to my teen mag days in the nineties, Chris O'Donnell was 'utterly swoonsome', and now a dad of five. He and LL Cool J (also a dad of five) were weekend highlights. Gary Sinise was charm personified, and who wouldn't want to spend 15 minutes in the company of *Magnum, PI*?

Everyone around the table had their list of people they needed to speak to. Mine was Marg, but I had a one-to-one with her later in the day, so I didn't need to panic.

Our group agreed that if one person had interest in whoever was put in of front of us but no one else did, the floor was theirs. If two people did, they would share the time going back and forth and so on.

If nobody required an interview with any of the above, we would go around the table each asking a question in turn to fill the time and not make anyone feel uncomfortable. Hey, talent, journalists are nice people too!

This is where your list of stock questions comes into play. Always be ready with a softball about their character, what they do in their time off, favourite smoothies, etc. You know the drill by now.

It worked like a dream. Everyone got what they needed, and we all had a nice chat with lots of lovely telly stars who we mined for spoilers although none were given.

Later in the day, after lunch which was a magnificent spread and eaten in a sunny courtyard, I sat down in a side room for my interview with Marg, who found huge fame playing feisty Catherine Willows in *CSI*.

I was also introduced to the show's executive producers Don McGill and Carol Mendelsohn, who I was intrigued to meet. Carol is one of those incredible women (along with Shonda Rhimes, Gale Anne Hurd, Jenji Kohan, and Ava DuVernay) who rule the entertainment industry.

She talked about the juggernaut that is the *CSI* franchise and said this to me, *"Every day we take a little time – we know what a remarkable thing it is, none of us could have done it alone. The right people keep coming along."*

I think some of that can be applied to navigating a roundtable. With the right people, it's going to be great. Take time to appreciate that.

One of the most memorable roundtables I was lucky enough to attend actually had a touch of the King Arthurs about it.

I was dispatched to Arundel Castle in West Sussex, to meet the cast of *Snow White and the Huntsman* which included Chris Hemsworth, Charlize Theron, Sam Claflin, Kristen Stewart, and Rupert Sanders, the director.

As junket locations go, Arundel Castle is impressive. It's a restored 11th century medieval castle and the principal seat of the Duke of Norfolk. It boasts magnificent views across the South Downs and the River Arun and original features such as a crenellated Norman keep. There's also a well tower, a stateroom, quadrangle, courtyard, and gardens. Inside you will find tapestries and paintings by van Dyck, Gainsborough, and Canaletto. It was a pleasant change from the Four Seasons.

Inside one of the grand dining halls the assembled press pack were shown to their tables, and there we waited to be served famous people who we talked to for an allotted amount of time about their new movie.

I'd interviewed Charlize and Kristen previously before, but Chris Hemsworth and Sam Claflin were both new to me. A couple of weeks before the junket by happy accident I'd had dinner with one of Sam's movement teachers from LACMA, his former drama school. She teaches Alexander Technique and so naturally her posture is immaculate. She'd asked me to say hello to Sam and after the interview before he was whisked away, I told him that Angie said hi. At the mere mention of her name he immediately sat up straight and I laughed. That's the incredible teaching power of Ms Herzberg.

The acoustics in the banqueting hall were fabulously bouncy so the atmosphere was electric, and the talent were all on top form.

Chris Hemsworth, who is as wide as he is tall, was charm personified. At the end of the roundtables while everyone else was led away to get their coaches back to London, I was told to wait at my table for Chris. He was going to do his one-to-one interview with me in the voluminous, echoey, wooden panelled dining room. I was the only journalist that day who got to meet Chris for a private chat. The interview was a lot of fun. There we were, Chris Hemsworth and I sitting in an empty medieval banqueting room, with just a handful of publicists watching from the balcony.

His mood was buoyant. His wife, Elsa Pataky, was about to give birth to their first child and as soon as we'd wrapped he was whisked away in a helicopter to a labour ward somewhere in London.

The former *Home and Away* actor told me of impending fatherhood: "*I don't think you can ever be completely ready but I can proudly say I'm now an expert at assembling changing tables, strollers, prams, and cots. And I've read all the baby books I can get my hands on.*"

I wished him well and he gave me a big *Thor* hug. Everyone who had been earwigging from the balcony swooned. (I worked on teen mags for years, so I know a good swoon when I hear one.)

I get it, he's a good-looking chap, most amenable and also the size of your local Tesco Metro. As a journalist it was memorable because his happiness and excitement in that moment was completely genuine. That's what you're looking for, authenticity.

In all, roundtables can be good for your health.

HEADLINES:

This is not a normal situation so be as normal as you can within its confines.

Communicate with your fellow roundtablers.

Don't hog the conversation.

Make eye contact and say hello to the talent when they walk into the room.

Don't go off on a tangent, keep your questions to the point.

Don't be afraid to get up from the table and change the a/c or heat settings.

Try to enjoy the alternate reality of the roundtable; famous people are literally brought to your table and they must talk to you. For many people this is living the dream.

CHAPTER 15

THE CHALLENGE OF THE PHONER

The world is a cruel place and often, for a myriad of reasons, you won't be able to interview a celebrity in person.

Chances are if you've got a staff job on a magazine, you'll barely leave your desk for days on end. You'll be reduced to eating endless bags of free Haribo and checking the Twitter feeds of the rich and famous just to get a celebrity fix.

This never used to be the case. Breakfast meetings and long lunches were the norm. I heartily recommend both, although not necessarily on the same day.

Despite my prehistoric credentials, I completely understand why, because of the ease with which you can converse with people online and a recent global pandemic, certain aspects of this job have changed beyond all recognition.

Putting COVID-19 aside (and don't we all wish we could), a lack of networking is a double-edged sword. Yes, you can save time by doing everything on email but leaving no time to meet people in person undermines the essence of the job.

Crucial relationships simply cannot be formed if there's no real connection. Cute emojis can't replace the joy of two spoons and one cheesecake. A well edited attachment will never replace your fourth round of tequila shots and a confessional that leaves you both bound together in blackmail and secrecy until the day you die.

What I'm saying is that authentic relationships establish trust. Hand-cuffing journalists to a desk might seem like a money saver but in the long run, all you're doing is hermetically sealing yourself inside a story-less bubble.

Also, what's the point of becoming a journalist if you're just going to sit at your desk all day? There are many other things you can do that require you to sit at your desk all day and they probably pay a lot better.

I've also noticed that many journalists now would rather eat their own eyelashes than actually pick up a phone. Stop this madness. If you can't leave your desk, at least make your vocal cords do some work.

In the interest of balance I'll say that I've interviewed many interesting people on the phone including the performance poet John Cooper Clarke (I sometimes listen to the recording just to hear him say the phrase 'lavish fenestrations' over and over again), Reese Witherspoon, Joanna Lumley, Adam Ant, Calista Flockhart, Dame Joan Collins, Kristin Davis, Kylie Minogue, Kevin McKidd, Julie Goodyear, Annie Lennox, and more soap and reality TV stars than you can shake a showbiz stick at.

There are also the ones that got away. I remember comedian and actress Victoria Wood cancelling a phone interview. I'm sad it didn't happen because she was one of my absolute idols and I wanted to tell her 'thank you', which would have been cheese on toast but I'd have done it anyway. She was a genius.

She didn't do many interviews and looking back at that particular time I think it's likely she cancelled because of her illness (which we didn't know about until she passed). Her loss was huge but frankly, we're lucky she was here at all. I don't have many regrets with this job – or indeed in life – but not talking to Victoria Wood is up there. That, and the fact I never married a Beastie Boy.

So while journalism is inherently not a desk job, sometimes you will have no choice but to do your interview over the phone.

The phoner, as it is universally called by those in the know, is the fast food of celebrity interviews.

Cheap, tasty, and sometimes destined to leave you with a bad feeling in your stomach depending on how digestible it is, the phoner can also be the most fun you'll ever have with an ear bug (the device you use to record an interview on the phone).

However, a phone interview strips you of everything visual so before you start you're already on the back foot. Because of this you will need to reach into your proverbial toolbox. Step away from your collection of IKEA Allen keys because your most important tool here is your voice.

Try this simple test:

Say the word 'Hello' out loud in your normal voice.

How did that sound?

Okay but a little flat?

Now say the word 'Hello' in your normal voice but while smiling at the same time.

Sounds different, right?

The smiley hello voice is the one you'll want to use on the phone when you're interviewing a celebrity. But not if you're interviewing anyone who is grieving or about to tell you a sad story. Use your common sense.

The tone of your voice will make a huge difference.
In Chapter Four, I talked about the energy you should give to the first 90 seconds after you walk into a room ahead of your interview with a famous person.

On the phone you get five seconds tops.

FIVE SECONDS, PEOPLE.

It's immediate. Your calling card is your voice and the first words you speak. And if that's not enough to get your attention think of your voice as the tool you're using to sell you. You are your own brand and used correctly, your voice can articulate the promise of a great interview.

A chipper greeting will always be preferable. Nobody wants to pick up the phone and hear the vocal equivalent of a dead battery on the other end.

This can be difficult sometimes, particularly if you're doing the interview in an office. It's always tough trying to be your 'interview self' while a room full of people are listening (even if they say they're not, you know they are).

Again, as with sitting front and centre at press conferences, I always try to lift my voice and just barrel through, sometimes being over loud in order to compensate for the fact that I wish I was at home or in a private room.

A whispered phone interview will never be as good as the one where you can really truly let yourself go. Brazen it out and imagine you're being so hilarious and captivating that you're doing everyone else in the office a favour by allowing them to listen.

Usually in an office this will require you to shout questions such as: 'SO EXACTLY WHEN DID YOU DECIDE TO GET VAGINAL REJUVENATION?', 'HOW LONG DID IT TAKE YOUR LABIA TO HEAL?' and naturally: 'WHAT'S YOUR FAVOURITE SMOOTHIE?'

Your other essentials are your research and your brilliant questions but there's also another element that may take time to perfect and that's the art of the conversation.

An interview is always a conversation but on the phone you have to ensure that it flows without too many interruptions or weird pauses. It's tricky to stop yourself from jumping into the dead space, especially if you know you need them to say more. You have to judge whether that pause is a real pause or a pause mid-thought. It can get confusing.

The worst of this is when there are five or six journalists on the line doing a 'phoner roundtable'. This set up is used for instances where journos need quick access so, for example, the morning after a *Big Brother* eviction. The publicist will put the evictee and several journalists on the line for their exit interview.

In this case you're all required to call into a conference line, state your name, and wait for everyone else to show up. Then it can be a real bun fight as the pack chips in with their questions. (Although sometimes more awkward if no one speaks.)

It's less than ideal but all you can hope is that you don't get an irritating phone hog and that the conversation flows without too many pauses.

Instinct should tell you whether to jump in and if the celebrity has just stopped talking for good, you'll soon know.

The worst is when you realise listening back to the tape that you've talked over a good answer or failed to follow-up on something they've said that's particularly interesting. Sometimes you'll get an answer to that follow-up if you email the publicist but many times you'll just have to suck it up.

A lot of pressure with a phoner comes with the time constraints. There is always a ticking clock. It's not always a bad thing but if I'm not using a desk phone or recorder which has a timer display on it, I start my iPhone stopwatch and place it directly in front of me. That way I can see very clearly how much time I have left.

Don't let anyone short-change you on minutes. It's irritating how little time journalists are given these days (in person and on the phone). Trying to spin a double page spread out of seven minutes can be tricky (sometimes fruitless) but not impossible. It's just better when there's more time. I would urge publicists to consider what the journalist has to go through to try to weave a story out of a ridiculously short interview. Does it always have to be quantity over quality?

"I have three minutes left," is all you need to say when you know you have three precious minutes left.

You can get a lot said in those minutes so fight for them.

The other pressure is the lurking presence of others.

Sometimes one, two, or maybe three people will be listening in on the line, maybe a combination of publicist, agent, or manager. You should be told ahead of the phoner if this is the case. They are usually on hand if their client is inexperienced, nervous, or in the news for some reason.

They are also likely to listen in if there is a product to promote. Crappy product promotion is the reason it feels like many celebrities, who by rights you should never hear from again after their show has been canned or their pop group has disbanded, are featured over and over in magazines.

Endorsements are one of the easiest ways for someone is who past their peak of fame to keep the money rolling in and stay somewhat relevant. A strong public profile is very important to a celebrity and these days social media has made it easier than ever for them to make a buck or two from peddling an atrocious diet product that might easily be called LITE-O DRINK. The celebrity in question needs to keep a high enough profile – and I'm talking lower level B or C list celebs here – in order that they might eventually get asked to join the cast of *Celebrity Spoon Making*.

Remember this when you're being given a hard time by an ego-driven human who you can't quite remember from doing that one thing that one time.

Recording their words while they're blatantly on the hustle and then printing their words accompanied by a big fat credit is you and your outlet doing them a huge favour.

This might sound cynical but don't give me a hard time on the phone if all we're here to do is make you another five grand and possibly get you cast in an afternoon antiques show all in the name of a questionable endorsement.

Often after you've asked your pre-agreed three questions about the diet shake, charity or event they're promoting you'll naturally want to move on to more interesting subjects such as the birth of their triplets or date with that recently divorced pop star. At this point the publicist is likely to jump in to ask you to stick to questions about the promotion.

Sigh.

An interview with a minor reality TV star gushing over LITE-O DRINK is singularly uninteresting and as a journalist you have a remit to deliver objective copy, get something at least approaching a new angle or story and not just roll out any old pap.

You don't exist to write advertorials (unless it's your job, then crack on), so you have to navigate these choppy waters and attempt to forge ahead with the content you know people want to read.

For certain publications questions are pre-approved to ensure that everyone knows what they expect. This kind of journalism is premeditated, sanitised, and utterly charmless.

Next time you pick up a celebrity magazine look for a chat that mentions a product or endorsement of some sort. It might be touched upon in the intro and there will be maybe one or two questions at the end of the piece that cover whatever it is ("I've never felt better than I do on LITE-O DRINK. Not only does it come with a free box of vitamins and doesn't in any way contain amphetamines, it's really changed my life!") and most likely an end credit telling you where you can buy this alleged miracle potion.

As you can tell I'm not a fan of celebrity endorsements (and certainly not diet drinks), pre-approved questions, or plugging any old crap just so a minor celebrity can holiday in Dubai. It's a necessary evil but I do feel that celebrities and PRs have more control over journalists than they deserve. I'd like to see the pendulum swing back the other way.

Sometimes though the pressure comes from the outlet you're working for. A couple of times I've done phone interviews on press day, knowing that the editor is expecting a quote for the cover and a quick turnaround. That's when a magazine starts to feel like a newspaper and things get exciting.

It's intense. You have to be very ready for the interview and know exactly what it is that you want and use every trick in the book to get it.

I once did a Katie Price interview for *OK!* and was given just five minutes with her. In that time, I had to get not just a one-page interview but also a good line that could be used on the cover.

I had my questions on the screen in front of me, including cover line suggestions, as well as printed out in front of me for extra comfort and 'glanceability', plus a notebook, pen, and a bottle of vodka. Sorry, water.

I probably had 20 panic attacks during that five minutes – all the while trying to keep my voice light and engaged – but I got the cover line and a story. Many journalists in the weekly market do this kind of thing all the time and are brilliant at it.

Travelling around the world and writing for so many outlets means that I've also worked remotely and across many time zones.

When I interviewed Annie Lennox for Oxfam's She Changes Lives campaign (for a piece that was published in a magazine in Australia), she was in New York and our phoner was set for 10.30 a.m. Eastern.

Meanwhile, I was in the desert in California and out the night before celebrating my boyfriend's birthday. That meant my phoner was set for 7.30 a.m. Pacific. That's a very early call time after an epic party.

All I remember is setting two alarms, being very worried that my mobile wouldn't get a signal in the desert (it was touch and go), and also being able to speak, read, or see.

Starting the phoner on the proverbial light and breezy note I soon cracked when Annie, who I've always been a huge fan of, mentioned how early it was for me.

I told her I'd had less than four hours sleep and was feeling a little delicate. She laughed, a gorgeous warm hearty laugh, and told me I needed to eat breakfast as soon as I put the phone down.

Explaining the situation at the start of the phoner, ahead of discussing some very serious issues, was actually a good call in this instance. It broke the ice. The interview went really well. No visual cues were needed. Just ibuprofen, a lot of water, and more sleep.

Another time, now perfectly sober and well rested, I interviewed a British personality on the phone and literally everything I said she took issue with, disregarded, or found a way to be as patronising as possible about. I don't know why she was so combative. Her phone manner was at total odds with her sunny public persona (therein lies a lesson). It was exhausting and demoralising. I won't say who it was in case you one day have the pleasure. When you do, you'll know, and then you can email me, and we'll exchange notes.

Just accept that sometimes you can't win.

The worst thing about the interview above was that I was working for a magazine who wouldn't have wanted me to write up the interview the way it happened. I had to make it sound like a happy little hug.

I'll be looking more at what happens when interviews go wrong in a later chapter because I've most certainly had my fair share of disasters but I just want you to know that sometimes, no matter how charming you are or how fair you're being, you may still end up with a stroppy celebrity and not getting the story you want. And we all want a good story.

You will also almost always be forced to sit by the phone waiting for the person to call, instead of calling them, and they will almost always be late.

I did a baby chat with *The Hills* stars Spencer Pratt and Heidi Montag, in 2017, for *OK!*, just a few short weeks after they'd welcomed baby Gunner. Fine, except that I was in the UK and they were in California. My alarm was set for 4.30 a.m. GMT, with the interview due to start shortly afterwards at 5 a.m., which would have been 9 p.m. PST.

There's nothing less glamorous than dragging your body out of bed in the middle of the night to talk about contractions and bodily fluids even if they are connected to the miracle of life.

Naturally, I'd prepared my questions the night before and also double checked the mobile phone number I was asked to call. I did some obligatory star jumps around the living room and made a pot of tea.

At the appointed hour I called the Speidi hotline, but nobody picked up. They didn't pick up for almost an hour and a half, by which time my second and third winds were long gone and I was beginning to wilt on the vine.

I emailed their publicist in the States who said she would find out what was happening. It turns out they'd fallen asleep and then the baby needed a feed. When we eventually got on the phone, they were very friendly. Spencer has the honour of being the first person to Snapchat one of my interviews, although I had to remind him as he was doing it that the interview was an exclusive and not give away too many details!

After we finished the hour-long chat, I checked all gadgets to ensure I had it all on tape (I did), sent an email to my editor to tell her it was in the bag and very entertaining, and then went back to bed for a couple of hours. I was shattered. It was such an early start and as the minutes ticked by, I was panicked at the thought of it not happening. It was utterly bleak.

Sometimes it won't be you who wants to get off the phone. I did a pretty cheerful phoner with Elizabeth Banks, while I was cat-sitting for friends in Marina Del Rey. It was for the 2011 movie *Man on a Ledge*, and just before Christmas. She was in her trailer in Baton Rouge, Louisiana filming *Pitch Perfect*, which she also produced, and was looking forward to going skiing with her family over the break. We zipped through the questions and the conversation stands out because of how I had two needy cats IN MY FACE the entire time I was on the phone, but also for how professional she was when she clearly had a massive to-do list to clear before the holidays. Sometimes it just goes well, and you don't even have to try too hard.

Before I put the phone down on you it's worth noting that because of COVID-19 you'll probably end up doing some of your interviews, including roundtables, via Zoom. It's harder to build a connection this way but not impossible. I noticed during lockdown that there was a real sense of "We're all in this together" and people were often more open. Find a decent background in your home and angle your camera in a way that's vaguely flattering (nobody wants to be distracted by your nostril hair). If I can, I avoid looking at myself on the screen as it's so distracting and oh my god how is it possible I now have so many chins?!

Don't panic about the tech as everyone has irritating issues that always seem to happen at the wrong moment. On Zoom recently I was forced to do an upgrade one minute before the meeting started, then for a completely random reason had to email out a new invite to everyone and ten minutes into the chat was forced to reboot my modem after the Wi-Fi randomly dropped. Stressful, but remember this can happen to everyone so keep your energy up and try to laugh about it. In some ways, a ridiculous tech disaster can be a bonding experience and don't forget to award yourself ten more points if you're a working parent and a kid does a cute thing halfway through.

And obviously, do remember to get dressed. Even your bottom half. The law of Zoom means that a delivery service will ring your doorbell mid-interview (that'll be the free LITE-O DRINK), and nobody wants to see your Paddington Bear pyjama-bottoms or see-through leggings. And if they do, I think you're reading the wrong book.

HEADLINES:

Your voice is your calling card. Make it sing! (not literally).
Set a timer so you don't get short-changed on time.
Try not to talk over anyone.
Relax into it, this is a conversation after all.
If you're on a conference call, don't hog the line.
Stay away from dodgy diet drinks.

CHAPTER 16

INTERVIEWS ON SHOOT DAYS

Newsflash. Much of what you see when it comes to the world of celebrity is make-believe.

Nobody looks magnificently coiffed, excessively flawless, or exquisitely styled within an inch of their life without a lot of help and many hours to spare.

As Kate Beckinsale told me when I commented on her immaculate appearance during our interview, "*It takes a village*."

Throughout my career, and particularly while living in Hollywood I saw at close quarters how the magic is made.

Living in a movie town is never dull. It wouldn't be unusual for a road to be blocked for shooting (and just to be clear I'm not talking about the gun kind, although roads were sometimes closed for that too, but for editorial or movie shoots).

I once went to grab a coffee at a café near my apartment in Atwater Village and couldn't get anywhere near it because

Law & Order were filming inside. Driving through downtown LA on a quiet Sunday morning I saw Bush's Gavin Rossdale writhing in a doorway shooting a video. I would say it caused my route to be diverted but if you've ever driven downtown, you know it has a mysterious road system that feels like you're on a constant diversion.

Memorably, I once went for a bike ride along the beach path only to be stopped in my tracks in Venice Beach by the sight of the Red Hot Chili Peppers performing on top of a low rise building near Muscle Beach. I loitered for a while because you know what, that doesn't happen every day.

I'm not saying you become inured to the madness of it all but one evening, fairly late, and having parked my car a block away from my apartment, I turned the corner to see a huge man, standing around 6' 4" in a checked shirt and dirty jeans, with a terrifying look in his eyes, carrying an axe and walking menacingly towards me with great intent.

My first thought was not the one that you would consider the normal reaction of a human being, i.e. "RUN FOR YOUR LIFE!" but instead, "I wonder what they're filming here tonight?"

Sure enough, I looked across the road to see a small crew crouched behind a car with one of them pointing a camera towards the murderous axe man.

"Terribly sorry," I said in that typically British way, when I realised I'd ruined the shot.

"Not a problem," he said with typical Californian ennui, as he walked back to first position.

On reflection, I knew in that moment that I'd probably been living in Hollywood for too long.

But where does this leave a journalist on a shoot day?

Shoot days can be a lot of fun but stressful for the journalist because photography always seems to take precedence over the words.

"Because it's a shoot day!" I hear you cry.

To which I say/shout, "WITHOUT WORDS NO ONE WOULD HAVE ANYTHING TO READ."

They are both important. I love and appreciate great photography and great photographers but we're not making picture books now, are we?

For convenience and scheduling purposes sometimes the only time a journalist will be able to chat to the talent is on the day the photos are being shot.

This is always tricky for the writer who somehow has to crowbar themselves into the day's proceedings when everyone else, including the publicist, photographer, their assistants, the stylist and make-up artist (and probably the talent themselves), no matter how nice they are, would rather you just piss off.

Essentially, there is no good time on a shoot day for a journalist to have an extensive heart to heart with the celebrity but that's exactly what you have to do. Prepare to navigate choppy waters.

At the start of the shoot it's all about hair and make-up; it's difficult to get stuck into a delicate subject when the talent is having their false eyelashes attached or being told by the make-up artist to close their mouth while they apply lip liner.

Once the shoot starts, the photographer is always loathe to stop if they're on a creative roll and at the end of the day everyone just wants to go home. Whatever way you spin it, the on-set journalist will always irritate someone.

And yes, it probably is incredibly annoying for everyone to stop working for an hour or more while the interviewer leaps in to do their thing but also, and here's the upside, it gives everyone a chance to eat their chicken Caesar or hummus wrap and take a little breather.

It's always easier if the shoot is at a location house because then you're in a contained environment but I've been on shoots in some interesting places.

Off the top of my head they include a polo field, rifle range, various locations on the streets of London, graffiti covered alleyways in LA, Runyon Canyon, the Las Vegas strip, Blackpool Pier, boats, fire engines, and trade shows.

I remember covering the Essex Show, a huge agricultural event and having to make a cow 'moo' in front of a crowd of onlookers so that the *Evening Echo* photographer could get the shot he wanted for the front page of that night's edition.

The headline was: "We are not a-moosed!"

Local papers are the best!

Shoot days are a unique beast. Think of it as the most annoying dinner party where all the guests have different dietary needs and yet somehow you need to produce a meal everyone loves. It takes a lot of effort.

With so many people, aside from yourself, trying to do the job they've been hired to do I've found that it's up to you, the journalist, to be the one who negotiates for the time and space they need. No one on a shoot day is going to be thinking about you or your story. That's your domain.

Even if it's written on the call sheet (the piece of paper that tells everyone where to be and when) what time you'll be sitting down for your chat, don't take it as a given that it will happen. Things change all the time on shoot days.

Luckily most photographers, make-up artists, and stylists are lovely people and very accommodating just as long as everyone knows what is going to happen and when.

My plan of action has always been to talk to the photographer at the start of the day to talk through the shots and figure out if there's a natural break for the chat to happen. The call sheet may say 11 a.m. but if we decide 2 p.m., then we can change it if it makes more sense. It always makes me less anxious to know what I'm doing and when, and it also helps the photographer to know he has, for example, three set ups before he gets to break for lunch while I do my thing. Clear communication really is the key to making everything work.

Sometimes you may have to start the chat while the celebrity is in hair and make-up, or even get it finished while they're sitting there if that's the only time you or they have that day. It's not ideal but you have to roll with the punches.

Travelling up to Manchester from the south of England for the day to interview Gemma Atkinson ahead of her appearance on *Strictly Come Dancing* in October 2017, I could only interview her before pictures while she was in hair and make-up. Because I had such a long journey, I simply couldn't stay to do it at the end of the shoot.

Another time I was invited to my first shoot with Miranda Kerr but only to observe and meet her ahead of our chat as her schedule was so tight. I did the interview on the phone later and it helped that we had met, albeit briefly.

Many times though I've found myself sitting in a celebrity's house at the end of the day, once the crew has left, having a nice chat in the kitchen over a cup of tea. It's just so much easier to interview someone when there's no one else around. Also, that's when the good biscuits come out and they can relax. I was even once invited by the sister of one rather lovely British celebrity to stay for their family Sunday roast (I said no but only because I had a long drive home).

When I arrive at the location, I always say hello to everyone because this is your crew. These are the people who are going to make shit happen. Without the co-operation of the people around you, you will be in big trouble. Learning the names of the photographer's assistant or the stylist is not just paying lip service to politeness, it's part of the job. Shoots are expensive so the more you can work as a team the better the job you will all do.

I introduce myself to the celebrity. Sometimes we've met before. Often times not, so again a good energy when you step into their orbit is crucial.

Even if you've had to traverse a perilous mountain range, sail across oceans, take six trains, four tubes, and a tram to get there in a snow storm and are on your period, pregnant, or suffering from a zinger of a headache, have had your house repossessed or your car rear-ended and would rather never speak to or see another human again, you have to somehow find a way to make it seem like you're having the time of your life.

My number one tip for anyone on a shoot day is to bring snacks. It used to be a given that any shoot you went on would be catered. Not any more.

In recent years I've been on shoots where the photographer has had to leave to buy sandwiches from the local garage just so everyone can get through the day without fainting.

Shoot days are always long. People need feeding. It's a massive irritation of mine when food isn't provided. It doesn't have to be a three-course meal but merely something nutritious enough to keep blood sugar levels up. This will ensure that the job is done well. In my mind, it's a false economy to not spend a few quid on a few salads, sandwiches, and fruit (plus milk for tea if you're working with Brits).

People get grumpy when they're hungry and that's when they lose concentration. On set there are cameras, cables and monitors that can be damaged or tripped over if people can't think straight because they're stuck in a mansion in a remote part of Cheshire or Simi Valley with no way of getting to a supermarket or café.

If you know it's going to be a long day, eat a hearty breakfast and then pack a sandwich/salad or grab one at the train station. Pack nuts, oatcakes, bananas, or whatever serves as your go-to energy burst. Always have something you can reach for. Losing brain power through lack of sustenance will sabotage your interview.

My next tip is somewhat unusual. Wear nice shoes but not shoes that are too new or too nice.

My friend, Laura Hills, who is now the deputy Head of Showbiz on the ITV daytime talk show *Loose Women*, but was then the Showbiz and Royal Editor on *OK!* magazine, has a cautionary tale. I'm going to let her tell it to you in her own words:

The shoot was in Knutsford, just outside Manchester, but there was a Tube strike on the London Underground and no direct trains, so it took me the best part of four hours to get there. My interview was with an early noughties girl band member, her fiancé and three children, and the location was in a gorgeous six bed location house in the middle of nowhere. With the shoot and interview over the celebrity said goodbye and I helped the photographer and stylist to pack up.

As I went to leave, at around 6 p.m., I noticed my brand new Nike trainers that I'd left by the front door were gone (the location house had a no shoes inside policy). With the help of the deputy picture editor I scoured the whole house, but they were nowhere to be seen. The only logical explanation was that the celebrity had picked them up by accident, so I quickly called her, but she insisted they didn't have them. With time ticking on and with a long journey ahead there was nothing for me to do but tie plastic bags around my feet and leave. To make matters worse, it was raining.

With 20 minutes until my train left for London, my taxi driver dropped me at the only store still open, Aldi, where I hobbled around the aisles in my plastic bag shoes until I found a pair of flip-flops. As I paid for them the checkout guy called all his colleagues over to check out "the latest fashion trend from London".

A few days later I heard from the celebrity's agent who revealed she had indeed taken them thinking they belonged to one of her sons. It took a further six months for her to return them to me and when I finally got them back, they'd clearly been worn.

You have been warned.

Expect the unexpected. Along the lines of making a cow moo I have – along with the rest of the crew – jumped frantically up and down behind the camera holding cuddly toys trying to make babies and toddlers look at the camera.

As the journalist on set this is not in your job description, but you want the pictures to look nice, right? And there's nothing funnier than watching half a dozen grown-ups flail around waving a rattle or Squishie gurgling, singing, or quacking like a duck just to get a baby to look cover-story perfect.

In the end newborns are the ultimate shoot saboteurs. If that baby isn't playing ball you will literally have no idea when the shoot will end or if you're going to get the shot. They always get in the way of the interview, even if the interview is about them and their birth story. Divas!

I remember sitting in a location house long after it had been booked out because the interview had to happen after the pictures. That took longer because the baby, who was only nine days old, needed to be breastfed after the interview. The now very tired celebrity mum and I felt like we were never getting out of there. Fortunately, the homeowners were most understanding.

The glory of shoot days is that you get to spend a good chunk of time in close proximity with people who you would never get to know in real life.

I was commissioned to interview Kris and Bruce Jenner for Australia's *New Idea* magazine. The shoot, in October 2011, was to take place at a location house in Tarzana, California, and the photographer was Nick Saglimbeni, who has photographed the Kardashians many times since 2007, including their Christmas cards and calendar shoots.

The brief was pretty simple: 'New Idea: *catch-up with Kris and Bruce Jenner in LA to talk about life as the parents of the most famous family in Hollywood! Along with married life and how they make it work, life as parents to the clan, and the day-to-day challenges that involves. Kris and Bruce will talk about their children, grandchild, and their relationships with them. They will also discuss how they both look so great and their diet, fitness and body secrets. As well as the launch of Kris' new book*!'

I was intrigued. Even though this was 2011 and a nudge pre-Insta and the influencer era, the Kardashians were already globally famous. I was curious to meet Kris, the world's most famous 'momager' who has made her family so rich I'm not sure there are enough zeros in the world to do their wealth justice.

I also remember Bruce from his sporting days. I have clear memories of my dad (a sports nut) and I watching him compete in the 1976 Olympics. Before interviewing Kris, and then the pair together, I was able to speak to Bruce solo, and told him a little story about me watching it with Dad and how we loved his performance. He seemed touched that I'd remembered he was once a high-profile sportsman. Then I ribbed him slightly by telling him how we'd enjoyed watching British decathlete Daley Thompson steal his gold medal in 1980 so much more. Thankfully, he found that very amusing. He was softly spoken and seemed gentle in spirit, which surprised me. At least, that was my takeaway from our conversation on that day.

Since this interview took place Kris and Bruce have separated, and Bruce has transitioned to Caitlyn (memorably announcing her name change on the cover of *Vanity Fair*). Remembering back to my day on set with Bruce, the news didn't surprise me as maybe it should.

The shoot had a coordinator so I was pretty much told what to do and when my interview would take place. After the introductions I stepped out of the way. There's nothing more annoying on set than an extra body who isn't needed. Never get in the way of anyone running around with equipment or step in front of a camera. Always be mindful of where the camera lens is pointing or where your shadow is falling if you're outside.

There were just three set ups that day so it didn't take long for the shots to be taken and then I had my 40 minutes with the Jenners.

I'd prepared for the interview within an inch of my life. I knew from reputation that Kris was all about business and I didn't want to be the idiot who arrived unprepared. I had everything I needed laid out in front of me and was laser focused.

I remember three details from the day itself.

First, I usually take snapshots with my phone on shoot days – as I've mentioned earlier – as visual cues. The shoot was taking place at the end of a long garden by the pool and I was staying out of the way in the kitchen. I snapped a quick photo on my BlackBerry (RIP) through the kitchen window. It was a blurry long shot of the Jenners and the photographer, who were all tiny, as I was so far away.

Somehow, the shoot coordinator saw me, sprinted back to the kitchen and berated me. She told me personal photographs were banned and that I'd been asked not to take any. I didn't know that and was slightly mortified at making such a faux pas.

At the same time, I didn't see the harm in it. It wasn't for publication and even though she asked me to erase the photo I didn't. Ha, rebellion! It's a blurry long shot and of no use to anyone but me.

Second, Henny heard I was meeting Kris and insisted I take a designer handbag to the shoot.

"Why?" I said.

"Because she'll notice," she told me.

I rolled my eyes.

I'm no fashionista as the Hermès tale illustrates. I don't particularly get fashion and I never notice labels. Henny selected a Tom Ford tote and said it was important I use it. I remember it being stiff and difficult to open.

The next day as I was being introduced to Kris, the first thing she said to me was, "Is that a Tom Ford?" I nearly died.

Thank you, Henny, in that instance you were right. Lesson learnt. Although I must emphasise that designer clothes and accessories are not in any way a necessary part of this job. Most people don't have that kind of cash (myself included), and not everyone is best friends with a stylist. Dress to feel confident in your own skin. Be you.

And the third was how professional and sharp Kris was (and also, that she had a rock on her finger the size of a small house). We had a great chat and covered everything the magazine wanted. I quipped at the end of the interview that I wanted to move in with her and the family so that she could manage my career. Jokingly she said she would adopt me. If that had happened I'd now have a new face, you'd all be wearing my eye shadow, and I'd be swimming in a gold-plated pool filled with Moët & Chandon. Dammit, why didn't I follow-up?

It was an easy day. Sometimes you expect people who are ridiculously famous to be awkward or aloof, but Kris and Bruce were neither. It was all about the business and getting the job done. For that one afternoon in October I liked them both. I still have that blurry photo somewhere and I'm glad I do. I don't, in case you're interested, have the expensive Tom Ford tote. I returned it the next day.

Shoot days are busy so when you do eventually sit down with the celebrity, and/or their family, you have to try to create a calm and intimate space.

This isn't always easy but try to find a room that people are not working in or walking through. If you're in a location house and there's a free living room (location houses are big and always seem to have two or three rooms with sofas in) that's always a good choice. Kitchen tables are also good but the kitchen is generally the magnet for everyone on a shoot and where the food will be (if you're lucky enough to have any).

Make sure they've eaten. Unless you're interviewing someone like Gemma Atkinson or Miranda Kerr, who are both devoted to health and fitness, it's easy for food to be forgotten by talent and many don't want to eat on shoot days because they want to look good in the pictures.

In 1994 I was working for a teen magazine called *BIG!* and was assigned to follow an up-and-coming model called Sophie Anderton. The brief was to describe her day as she went along to various shoots, appointments, and jobs. Many times you never hear of up and comers again but less than two years later Sophie landed a high-profile Gossard bra campaign and became very famous.

She was only 17 the day I met her and just starting out. Our day (featuring myself, the magazine's art director, and photographer) began before 8 a.m. when we called for her at her flat in central London. We waited a long time for her to appear and then trailed her on two shoots and finally an evening catwalk show. It was a long day. By the end of the second shoot – at this point it was late afternoon – I asked her if she'd eaten anything and she said no. I remember virtually blocking her way out of the kitchen insisting that she ate at least a slice of toast, which she did with a tiny slick of peanut butter. I can't do anything without food in my belly and was worried she would collapse after such a long and physical slog. She seemed relieved to have someone in front of her telling her to eat. But it was one slice and that was it.

It's not part of my job to ensure people are fuelled up but I can't help myself. I did a shoot with a model in LA who was showing clear signs of anorexia. I emailed her agent to outline my concerns but never heard anything back. Agents have a duty of care and I thought they needed to know. Modelling is a different universe, I know that, but at the end of the day we're all human, and we should be looking out for each other.

Side note to the Sophie Anderton day: *I've never seen a woman affect traffic the way she did. As we walked down the street in west London cars and humans slowed down to look at her. Men did double takes and literally stopped in their tracks. It took me a while to work out what was happening as Sophie seemed as oblivious as she was stunning. That was the day I realised without a shadow of a doubt that I had to make a successful career as a writer.*

Timing is everything. On shoot days you will be more keenly aware of the clock than the white rabbit in *Alice in Wonderland*. In fact, that furry little bunny had it easy compared to you.

Even after you've created your intimate space, you will never forget that there are probably 12 people milling around with nothing to do because you're holding the stars of the show hostage. There will also be people shooting behind-the-scenes footage for online who are desperate to be in there with you. To all these people you are officially the devil incarnate.

By now you will have read your brief, done your research, and prepared your questions in an order that makes sense to you and the story. You will have dispensed with small talk before sitting down because you have to crack on at the speed of light. Sometimes you can grab another 10 or 15 minutes later in the day but that isn't a given.

When the subject matter is weighty, I'll usually talk them through the subjects we are covering beforehand so that there are no surprises. Sometimes the content of the interview has been agreed beforehand, and even written into the contract, so asking the tough questions shouldn't be a problem.

If the agreed interview time is an hour, take the full hour, and get everything you need.

Afterwards, while you still have the talent close to hand, go through your questions and notes, and then ask any follow-up questions while they're still in easy reach.

It's always worth checking your emails to see if there are any messages from your editor, who may have thought of something else to include while the interview was happening.

Afterwards, check your recording devices and jot down any interesting details from the day that you may wish to add into the piece for colour.

You might be having so much fun that you'll want to stick around and see how the rest of the shots pan out. I love being on set so I'll always stay longer unless there's a train to catch, or the deadline is so tight I need to crack on with the writing.

Then it's time to leave the magic-making to everyone else.

HEADLINES:

Pack enough snacks to see you through the day.
Bring good energy with you to the set.
Communicate with the photographer and team.
Don't get in anyone's way.
Take all your interview time, don't be rushed.
Be flexible, anything can happen on shoot days.
Never wear new shoes and if you do, don't take them off.

CHAPTER 17

WHEN IT ALL GOES WRONG

I'm sitting in my car outside my apartment in Hollywood. It's a scorcher of a day and the sweat running from my back could solve California's drought problem.

I'm waiting for my mobile to ring as I'm about to interview Reese Witherspoon ahead of the release of her new movie, *Water for Elephants*.

I'm having a literal meltdown because it's so hot. I can't do the interview inside my nice, cool apartment because there's no phone coverage inside.

Top tip: *When renting an apartment, check that you can send and receive calls inside its four walls as this is extremely useful if you're a journalist, and also generally in real life.*

The countdown to the phoner has begun so at this late stage my car is the only place I can think of which is sheltered, nearby, and quiet enough for me to do a cover interview.

In a rush I toss my notebook and recorder onto the passenger seat before turning the engine over and cranking up the barely effective aircon. Just then, my phone rings. It's Reese. I hurriedly fix the ear bug into my ear (where else?) and attach the other end of the wire to my recording device. I can see that the red light of my recorder is on and so the interview starts.

For a swelteringly hot car phoner it doesn't go too badly.

Reese is chatty. When she finds out I'm only a mile from her home, she asks why I didn't come to visit her in person, as if I could have requested it like I was popping in to see a friend.

I'm frantically scribbling notes as we talk because the line isn't particularly good and an after 40 minutes, we say our goodbyes.

It's only then that I notice I've stuck my ear bug into the outlet that says 'ear' and not 'mic' meaning that I haven't caught any of what she said on tape.

My stomach lurches.

This is a cover story.

I listen back to the conversation and all I can hear is my own voice.

"So, Reese, how did you find riding an elephant?"

Silence, then, "Yep…uh-uh…oh really…20 feet…that's high…amazing…uh-uh, great…wow, you must be very flexible…"

On and on and on.

Me and no Reese.

Crap.

I look down at my notepad and see that I've scribbled notes in both shorthand and longhand. After a quick mental calculation, I figure there's enough to make the piece happen.

I get out of the car along with a Niagara Falls amount of water streaming down my body and race back inside the apartment to "transcribe" what I have using the notes and audio cues of my questions, plus my reactions to her answers. Thankfully, my memory is still pretty sharp too.

Like a whirling dervish I get the interview written up as quickly as I can. Time is of the essence and I don't want to lose any nuance or quote.

More importantly, I don't what to be that idiot who has to call the publicist and tell them I need to do the interview again (something that would be unlikely to happen).

Some of what Reese says is slightly paraphrased but nothing is made up or veers away from our conversation.

After three hours, I reckon I'm good to go. I send the copy over to my editor in Australia and wait for them to email back saying, *This has clearly been written from memory and chance, you utter charlatan*!

But no, nothing. They run the story with barely any edits or additions.

I got away with it that time but only because I wrote down those copious car notes.

But the main thing I didn't do, apart from record the interview, was panic.

Those scribbles and shorthand notes saved the day.

Since "The Reese Incident", as I now call it, I've always double checked that my ear bug has gone in the right hole. Sounds gross, but it works.

Sometimes, however, events take on a life of their own and things go wrong in this job so spectacularly you simply have to ride the wave.

I now present to you "The Denholm Diaries", a story told by my friend Julie Seddon, who I've mentioned in this book earlier. This happened while we were working on the local paper together.

For background, Denholm Elliott, who died aged 70 in 1992 from AIDS related tuberculosis, was a renowned

British character actor best known for his work on *Raiders of the Lost Ark*, *Trading Places*, *A Room with a View* (for which he was nominated for a Best Supporting Actor Oscar), and the TV series *Bangkok Hilton*.

At the time of Julie's interview, Denholm's daughter, Jennifer, had been making her own headlines; according to the now defunct tabloid, the *News of the World*, she'd turned to prostitution to fund her heroin addiction (she took her own life in 2003). The story was extremely sad, and this is sometimes a dilemma of journalists who are sent to talk to stars who may be in the news for reasons other than whatever it is they're plugging. You are required to ask the questions to move the story along.

But while it is expected you will ask them, the person you're talking to doesn't necessarily have to answer them.

This is what happened to Julie:

In the summer of 1988, the film Killing Dad was being made in Southend-on-Sea, starring Julie Walters, Richard E Grant, and Denholm Elliott. Our paper, The Evening Echo, was invited to send a journalist to interview the three on set. I was very keen to interview Julie Walters because I loved her work with Victoria Wood who was from Bury, as I am, and I was also keen on interviewing Richard E Grant whom

I thought was a fascinating actor. I wasn't that interested in Denholm Elliott, which is lucky considering what happened. I volunteered to go and as no one else wanted to do it, I was given the job with the direction from the news editor: "Ask Denholm Elliott what he thinks about the News of the World story on his daughter being a prostitute to buy drugs." Not a problem.

I interviewed Julie Walters on Southend Pier and she was lovely. It was more of an informal chat and as we talked, I noticed Denholm Elliott standing off to one side smoking and giving us dirty looks. He didn't look happy.

The interview with Elliott was next and Richard E Grant was to be the last one. I was disappointed as I would have preferred to talk to Grant next but was taken to Elliott's trailer by a PR woman and was left with him.

There was also another journalist from a weekly paper and while we had interviewed Walters individually, Elliott had insisted we both interviewed him at the same time.

He chain-smoked throughout the interview and answered our questions with just a single word or two. He was very difficult to engage with so the interview wound down and finally I asked the last question, 'How did he feel about the News of the World *story about his daughter turning to prostitution to feed her drug habit?'*

I expected him to talk about how the NoW *shouldn't have published the story; how it was a private family matter; or even about the difficulties of their children's drug addiction on the parents.*

He actually went berserk. He started screaming at the top of his voice and sprayed spittle as he yelled. I was – literally – seeing someone foam at the mouth. I tried to apologise and said, "I'm sorry I had to ask." He continued shouting about the media and I repeated, "I'm sorry I had to ask." Looking back, I think he thought that I was insisting on an answer when actually I was trying to apologise for upsetting him.

He shouted we should get out, so we left and found the PR woman at the bottom of the steps of the trailer, having heard the noise. "He's a bit upset about something I asked him," I told her. Elliott appeared in the doorway and shouted at her, waving his arms, then slammed the door. She told us to leave the set straight away and so – thrown off a film set – I never got to interview Richard E Grant, which was a pity.

The director and producer immediately thundered along to the newspaper's offices to complain about me, how I'd upset a Great British Actor so much he had locked himself in his trailer and couldn't film for the rest of the day. They also wrote a letter of complaint to the editor who showed it to me with the words, "Who do they think he is – Laurence Olivier?"

Do I regret asking that question? No. It was a reasonable question to ask about the impact of a news story on him and if he'd have behaved professionally and said "no comment" we would have moved on.

I did learn a lot from this. When I moved into PR, I always made sure the journalist knew what questions were off limits; I discussed in advance with the interviewee what the response would be if the journalist asks them (they usually do at the end, as I did!) and I would never let someone be interviewed on their own without my being there to make sure everything goes smoothly.

It doesn't go more wrong than being thrown off a movie set. It's never happened to me so I thank Julie for sharing her story. In my opinion she didn't do anything wrong. She was doing her job. Some celebrities need to be managed a little more than others. Just because a journalist asks a question doesn't mean the celebrity has to answer it.

Also, given the nature of local papers back in the day, her being thrown off the set in such dramatic fashion was regarded in the office as a badge of honour. Frankly, the story has gone down in local paper lore.

Before we leave this anecdote, it's worth mentioning that the other journalist in the trailer that day sold the story about Julie being thrown off the set to *The Express* newspaper, thus thrusting her momentarily into the spotlight. Apart from that though, Julie survived pretty much unscathed.

There are some more uglies. I've seen a world-famous actor make a journalist cry before. Not a trainee but a grown man with a few years in the job under his belt.

I won't name the actor in question because I have a feeling he'd sue me for all the money I don't have.

At an international press junket, he took offence when a Japanese journalist asked him about the character he was currently playing in a long-running drama. The show had just been released in this journalist's territory and he didn't know too much about it. For the sake of his readers, he wanted the actor to introduce the character in his own words.

The actor, who was a big star, was so rude and unpleasant in his response that the Japanese journalist started to shake with fear. The actor was affronted that the interviewer didn't know more about the show (that hadn't aired in his country yet). If you know the slightest thing about Japanese culture, you will know how wonderfully kind, polite, and proper they are. The last thing this journalist wanted to do was upset the star of the show.

The actor's response was completely unreasonable and unnecessary. It was a roundtable but as I recall, there was no actual physical table. So it was that rare beast, the naked roundtable.

He sneered his way through the rest of the questions and then dramatically stomped off as we all looked on in mild shock and utter disdain.

The publicist turned to us in horror. She was apologetic but we knew it wasn't her fault.

The overwrought Japanese journalist burst into tears and we tried to console him. He couldn't work out what he'd done wrong and we tried to explain that he'd done nothing improper or rude.

The bottom line was that the actor was a ridiculous man baby and I'll never watch anything he's in ever again (or has been in, which cuts out a franchise I used to love). I can barely look at him now if he pops up on my screen and not think of his mean comments and stompy exit.

There's not a lot you can do when a celebrity is that unpleasant except move swiftly on.

The most dramatic stories, if they surface, always get more press. In 2015 it was reported that Channel 4 presenter Krishnan Guru-Murthy offended Robert Downey Jr on camera with a question about his addictions.

Sensing that the actor was confused at his line of questioning, Guru-Murthy explained, "*The reason I'm asking you about the past is that you've talked in other interviews about your relationship with your father and the role of all of that in the dark periods you've been to, taking drugs and drinking and all of that. I'm wondering if you're free of all of that or if that's something you…*"

To which Robert Downey Jr cuts him off, saying, "*I'm sorry, what are we doing?*"

He then gets up and leaves the room.

While it's not an ideal scenario, it got Channel 4 news and Krishnan Guru-Murthy a ton of press. That's the way it goes sometimes.

It's up to you to decide whether you think the interviewer pushed the boundaries. I don't think he did in this instance. People talk a lot about invasion of privacy but this was an interview that had been given the green light and Robert Downey Jr is an actor with a rich and complicated history. It's well within a journalist's remit to ask.

After that it was up to RDJ to decide if he wanted to be there or not.

He didn't, so fair enough. Or not?

You can find the exchange online and make up your own mind.

In 2015, at the Toronto International Film Festival, the actor Tom Hardy shut down a reporter at a press conference who asked him about his sexuality (fairly tenuously), in relation to his role in the Kray brothers movie, *Legend.*

He actually says, "*What on earth are you on about*?" To which there is a smattering of laughter around the room.

There is some back and forth before he says, "*Are you asking me about my sexuality?*"

The reporter says, "*Sure.*"

Tom Hardy replies, "*Why*?" Followed by a polite, "*Thank you.*"

And that was the end of that.

Press conference over.

I would suggest that if you're going to talk to a star about their sexuality, a press conference is not the place to do it. You have to at least try to establish a sense of context and some kind of rapport to be able to comfortably dive talk on those terms.

I mentioned before that I once interviewed a female personality over the phone and that she disagreed or took umbrage with everything I said.

It was exhausting but you just have to push on through and then collapse on the sofa afterwards.

The irony is that her on-screen persona is the absolute opposite to the one I encountered. She's another one who if I accidentally hear her voice or see her on the television, I break out in a cold sweat and immediately switch off.

It's also annoying beyond belief when people don't call at the allotted time or disappear from the face of the earth completely but again there's nothing you can do in that situation apart from chase the PR (or whoever is your contact) and let your editor know.

You are not the celebrity's keeper. It should never be your fault if an interview doesn't happen because someone else hasn't kept their end of the bargain.

Sometimes things happen that are so far leftfield there's no way you can see it coming.

I was once mid-interview with an easily recognisable actress at a beach-front hotel in Santa Monica when she started her period. She was wearing an all-white suit at the time. She told me what was happening and then ran to the en suite bathroom. I scrabbled around in my bag for a tampon, but it was a new work bag (non-designer) and I didn't have one.

Knocking on the bathroom door I told her that I was going to look for her assistant, who eventually took care of it. I wandered off for a bit and ten minutes later she was back on the sofa, brushing it off as if it was nothing. It wasn't a big deal, but we did joke about her wearing all white.

"This won't go in the article, will it?" she asked, laughing at the absurdity of it all.

I assured her it wouldn't and to this day I've never told anyone the identity of the menstruating movie star, so don't bother asking.

Although in a quality side note: *later that day my editor called to say she'd heard that the actress in question was pregnant. For once in my life I could categorically tell her that no, she wasn't. *punches air with joy at not getting it wrong for a change**

So yes, things will go wrong. Sometimes a bit wrong and sometimes badly wrong.

Chances are you'll still get a good story out of it anyway.

If you don't tape the interview then yes, that's your fault but mostly, when it comes to the foibles of celebrity, it won't be your fault.

Keep calm and carry on said someone once, and they were right.

HEADLINES:

Don't panic.
Stay calm.
Breathe through whatever explosions are happening around you.
Don't be afraid to reach out to a publicist or editor.
All things will pass.
It will be okay.

CHAPTER 18

SHINE ON CAMERA (IN THE RIGHT WAY)

Saturday, 15th December 2012.

Dear TV Journalist,

You've been APPROVED to participate in the international TV interviews at the GANGSTER SQUAD Worldwide Press Day from Friday, December 14th – Saturday, December 15th at the Four Seasons Hotel in Los Angeles.

That's me! I am Dear TV Journalist!

Today is the day. The Holy Grail of days. The Drive of days, the day *La La Land* became a reality. The day a Half Nelson became a full Nelson. The day my own notebook said hello to the star of *The Notebook* ("That's enough now," – Ed.)

Today is the day where I finally get to answer the interminable question of questions, "What's Ryan Gosling like?"

Turns out, after all my years as a celebrity interviewer in Los Angeles I didn't bump into Ryan in the coffee shop, art gallery, goat Pilates, or karaoke night at a pub in Santa Monica (don't laugh, that's how I got to hang out with the late Davy Jones of The Monkees, who jumped out of nowhere to join a random woman in a couple of rousing choruses of 'Daydream Believer').

No, I was nominated and approved for an on-camera interview with him for *The Guardian*. Not the meaty in-depth profile I was aiming for but I'll take it.

It's bitter-sweet. *Gangster Squad* is my last junket of the year, and also my last in LA before heading back to the UK.

But still, it's Gosling.

Ryan Gosling. Ryan. Sir Ryan of Gosling, Ry-Ry, the Canadian swoonster, the Gosmeister ("Stop it!" – Ed.)

We won't be shooting the breeze and slapping each other on the back like old pals. And I certainly won't have time to peel back many layers or dig deep. No such luck. This is an on-camera interview and the schedule is tighter than one of those latex creations that Babs' friend Kimberly squeezes herself into.

Interviewing Ryan is not the only job I have that day. After the *Gangster Squad* interviews (I'm also talking to Emma Stone, Josh Brolin, and director Reuben Fleischer), I'm scheduled to do a one-to-one print interview with Mila Kunis for *Oz The Great and Powerful* for *Sunday Magazine*.

Typically, in something like that soggy boating scene in *The Notebook*, it never rains, but it pours.

But I digress.

It's LA so my working day starts at 4.30 a.m. I blend a green vegetable juice then spend an hour in the gym with my personal trainer before a hike around Runyon Canyon, followed by a guided meditation as I focus my thoughts with my flexitarian life coach, who also doubles up as my Botox technician.

Joking!

My day starts at 6 a.m. with a hot shower, a bite of a stale Trader Joe's pretzel bread stick, and a pit stop for a giant dirty coffee filled with 28 vanilla mini milks from the 7/11 (it was a phase I was going through, don't judge). This breakfast of champions is followed a stressful crawl across Hollywood in solid traffic to the Sony lot in Culver City to view the new *Oz* footage.

I love visiting the lots and the Sony one is particularly fine because of its history and art deco buildings.

Singin' in the Rain was shot here in 1952, the train interiors from *Some Like It Hot* were shot here by Billy Wilder in 1959, part of *Jaws* was shot here in 1975, as were *Ziegfeld Follies*, *Ben Hur*, *North by Northwest, Rocky, Jerry Maguire, Men in Black*, *Cast Away, Interstellar,* and fittingly, *The Wizard of Oz* in 1939.

The studio was built in 1918 by brothers Harry and Jack Cohn. Harry went on to found Columbia Pictures and was much feared in Hollywood for his ruthless deal-making, short temper, and long memory. He also expected his female actors to sleep with him for roles. Remind you of anyone?

Curiously, my dad held the theory that Harry Cohn was his uncle. He once told me that his mother was a twin and that her brother was adopted. Baby Harry was apparently sent to live with a family New York because their parents couldn't afford to keep both babies.

Apart from the fact that my grandmother, Annie, was a twin who was separated from her brother, I've found absolutely no evidence that the rest of this story is based on anything but my dad's wild imagination. He was a movie lover who also loved to spin a yarn.

The *Oz* footage was pretty good. But there was no time to hang about and muse about Munchkins or 'great uncle

Harry' as I had to jump back in my car and drive back across town to Beverly Hills to my old fave, the Four Seasons.

Ahead was the series of on-camera interviews with the *Gangster Squad* cast and its director. This was to be the scene of the crime, if you will. (Or not. I don't care, we're almost at the end of the book.)

On-camera interviews are even more anxiety-inducing than one-to-one print interviews. You have absolutely no time to draw breath, peel back layers, or form any kind of meaningful connection with your interviewee.

There are generally so many journalists scheduled per celebrity that you may have as little as three to five minutes to get into the room, do your bit, and leave.

It's the most glamorous of sausage factories. A conveyor belt of content.

As always preparation is key but there's more to think about when you're on camera. I've also done some on-screen punditry but have mainly kept my face behind the camera as being in front of it is such a palaver.

You need to look fabulous; your wardrobe needs to be fabulous, and your hair and make-up needs to be double fabulous. You also need a lot of it. For a pre-Oscars on-camera punditry gig I hired a make-up artist friend to give me the full works. False lashes, the lot. I've been around make-up artists a long time now and I'm still amazed at how they're able to transform a face. They are geniuses, no doubt about it.

Gangster Squad was a little different in that I didn't have the luxury of time to prepare, pamper, and preen.

I was also due to leave the States a couple of days later and was in the middle of packing up an apartment and my belongings. Everything felt rushed, last minute, and haphazard. Truth be told I felt queasy at the thought of the day ahead.

For the interview I wore trusty favourites; skinny jeans, crisp shirt, and jacket, and threw my make-up bag in with my recorders and research so that I could add more colour to my lips and cheeks later. There was no guarantee that my face would end up on camera. Many times, journos are edited out (and that ultimately, thank goodness, was the case with this interview).

So while I felt as if I was prepared earlier in the day, the rush to get to the point at which I found myself sitting opposite Ryan left me sweaty, harried, and ill at ease. Not ideal. Where was my flexitarian life coach when I needed them?

After checking into the junket, I found my brilliant journalist friend James White, who was there doing the same job as me but for *Empire* magazine. We sat in the corridor outside the suite where Ryan was being interviewed. It's like a dentist's waiting room but with cleaner carpets and better upholstery.

Being an old hand at this type of thing he gave me one note: don't get up from your chair before they unclip your mic.

Noted.

As we sat in the corridor, crew from the shoot dashed back and forth while publicists talked urgently into walkie talkies. I'd told *The Guardian* that I would deliver the memory cards (how the data was stored back then) to them in person as I was flying back to London that same week.

I'd seen the movie the day before at the Chinese Theatre, on Hollywood Boulevard. It was an okay film. Not great but I liked the way it looked and as Ryan and Emma proved in both *La La Land* and one of my favourite movies this millennium, *Crazy, Stupid, Love*, they have fantastic chemistry.

In a quiet moment I went over my questions.

You have to start strong with an on-camera interview. No closed questions that will elicit only a yes or no.

Feeling all sorts of panic and a sudden extreme tiredness I dabbed my shiny face with powder and added more lippy just as my name was called. I was told in no uncertain terms by a harassed human wearing all black that I had only five minutes in the room and couldn't go over UNDER ANY CIRCUMSTANCES.

Five minutes when you're doing a plank in the gym feels like 20 years. Five minutes in a junket shoot is a nano-second.

Then the harassed human said the magic words, "*Ryan is ready for you now.*"

My stomach lurched. Was it nerves or the 7/11 vanilla mini milks coming back to haunt me?

Entering the room I gave myself a short, sharp inner talking to about energy levels.

"This is what you wanted, Marks!" and walked purposefully forward, almost tripping over a camera tripod that had been placed in front of the door to the suite.

Suddenly, bathed in the light of what seemed like a thousand movie lamps, there he was looking slim, handsome, and well, surprisingly festive.

Ryan Gosling was wearing a Christmas jumper.

I suddenly felt less tired. There's nothing like a seasonal knit to warm the cockles.

I smiled my staple wide junket hello and shook his hand as I introduced myself. He smiled back and yep, there it was, the charm you've seen splattered all over the movie screen.

This is how they reel you in, these wily movie stars.

Their wattage is greater than everyone else's. Even Ryan's low-key, "Hello, nice to meet you," was great and powerful (to borrow from the other movie that day).

But still, there was a job to do.

As I sat down a sound man wearing a headset appeared out of nowhere and asked if he could fit me with a microphone.

He clipped it on and once I'd checked my voice levels, I skimmed my page of notes and tried to look as calm as I possibly could. There were three cameras set up in the room. One on me and two on Ryan (quite right).

Ryan was relaxed. He probably had 20 more of my ilk to see that day and wasn't about to expend any more energy than necessary.

I waited for the director to yell action although that's over-egging it a bit. To be honest, it was more like a grunt of, "Okay go."

And I was off.

It's important to keep the tone of your voice up on camera. When I watch the clip back, I think I sound flat and a little short of breath and can only put that down the insanity of life at that time. Not a great excuse though. You can't allow things like that to throw you off course. You have to be there in the moment.

You should also avoid talking over the celebrity as that will screw up the edit. You need clean soundbites. Your editors won't be able to use anything you mumble over, so keep yourself in check when it comes to saying anything at all. At the same time do your best to make the conversation seem natural.

Yes, you're walking a tightrope and the clock is ticking but shhhh, let them do most of the talking.

And unless you're a natural performer, you have to block out the fact that 20 people might be watching you. That's not always easy either.

Staying focused in this situation is everything.

I knew I had certain beats that I wanted to hit but I also wanted to get in a little bit of personality and so after talking about the movie, I brought up the fact that he was wearing a Christmas jumper. He made a quip about it, I laughed and in a flash the interview was over.

Then, like a complete idiot, I stood up still wearing my mic. Doh.

The cable yanked me back down. The weary tech guy rolled his eyes as he unclipped me.

Ryan sat there smiling and said something along the lines of, “We’ve all done it,” or he could have said, “Kettle, magnet, pancake.” Truth be told, I wasn’t really listening to the movie star through my thudding embarrassment.

After I said goodbye to Ryan and the crew, I asked someone else, also dressed in black, where I could find the room to pick up my memory cards. I scurried along the corridor to the hospitality suite wondering what the hell had just happened.

For me, it wasn’t the best but on the plus side, I didn’t have anything to write up. I just had to do it three more times and then I was free to leave for my interview with Mila.

I can’t remember an awful lot about my interview with director Reuben. The chat with Josh went well because he remembered I’d stolen his cigarettes at the *Wall Street: Money Never Sleeps* junket in New York, so we’d already established some kind of face and nicotine recognition, and Emma, who I’d never met before, was very personable.

Every time I finished the interview, I stood up wearing my mic.

Every. Single. Time.

I'm better at this kind of malarkey now but I'd advise that if you want to be on camera, you should get professional training. The journalism side is one thing but presenting yourself as camera ready is another skill entirely.

Thanks to my talented and creative community, I always had lots of help but looking good, sounding good, and not showing yourself up to the world as you do the job is no mean feat. You should learn as much about camera craft as you can if that's the direction you want to go in.

We are now living in a world of content and influencers, and it's important to know how to present yourself to edge out the competition. You need to show you have a brain and a personality, and you have to be able to think on your feet. You can't just be a generic head covered in wacky filters and bunny ears.

After all the interviews were finished, I collected the memory cards, stashed them in my bag, said goodbye to the PR team and grabbed a Danish from hospitality (pastry not a human). I hurried downstairs to retrieve my car from the valet ahead of the 40-minute drive to the Luxe Sunset Boulevard Hotel.

Time was marching on and my interview with Mila Kunis was scheduled for 4 p.m. I'd never been to the Luxe and got lost trying to find the entrance to the hotel but thankfully I arrived there with around 20 minutes to spare.

I checked in, grabbed another coffee and probably some other kind of sugar-laden snack, and sat down with my *Oz* notes. Time to switch gears.

Before I met with Mila in one of the conference rooms, I was told I couldn't mention her relationship with Ashton Kutcher, which was pretty new at that time. I didn't bring it up, but we did talk about her almost festive cream, woolly jumper. In hindsight, it was a day for good knitwear.

Note to anyone non-American visiting the States during winter; if you call a jumper a jumper they'll think you're talking about overalls, so use the word sweater. This saves a lot of explanation and time-wasting especially during an interview when the clock is ticking.

I wrapped up my chat with Mila and headed home via the pastry table promising myself that a vegetable would most definitely figure in my near future.

As I sat on the 10 freeway, I pondered over my all too fleeting meeting with Ryan. When people ask you about someone so many times you need to be prepared with the answer.

But the truth is there wasn't that much to tell.

How did Ryan smell? Not of peanuts as I mused earlier. He smelled of nothing strident so basically, he smelled okay.

He was low-key nice.

I asked questions and he answered them. We did the job. He did his bit and I did mine.

There's not much more to it than that. And the reason that I can't be more detailed is that I didn't really get to know him.

I just sat in front of him for five minutes.

Which brings us full circle. I didn't form any kind of meaningful relationship with Ryan Gosling, I merely did what I was in the room being paid to do on the day.

Yes, his celebrity smile was cheeky and infectious, and yes, we laughed about Christmas jumpers/sweaters but only in the name of content.

I admit, I'd love another interview with him. A proper chunky, full-fat, no limitations conversation. But if I don't get it, then that's okay too because at least now I have an answer to the age-old Ryan question.

SCENE

"Lisa, what's Ryan Gosling like?"

"He was easy to talk to but has questionable taste in knitwear."

END SCENE

There you go. That's what Ryan Gosling is like.

I played that interview, and the others from that day, over and over in my head. I did okay, I think. It's hard when it all happens so fast and you can't see the footage or do your own editing (*The Guardian* do that in-house).

The 3.29-minute clip they uploaded to the website was snappy and made me sound like I knew what I was talking about. As of publication, it's still on their film site if you want to seek it out.

The blurb reads: *The stars of Ruben Fleischer's fictionalised account of the battle against mob boss Mickey Cohen tell Lisa Marks why violent policing blurs the line between the good guys and the gangsters – and how making a film set in 1940s Los Angeles can help you quit smoking.*

Smoking? Surely not in LA where health is paramount.

Fatigued but feeling pretty good about life, I hopped off the freeway and noodled my way home, stopping once to pick up a large salad from the grocery store.

It was time to finish packing my suitcases and leave Hollywood.

For the time being anyway…

HEADLINES:

Dress well, do something fabulous with your hair and if you don't have time for full on make-up, then at least get rid of the shine.

Keep your questions short, interesting, and open ended.

Wait for the celebrity to answer in full before talking.

Never stand up wearing your mic.

Eat your vegetables.

CHAPTER 19

"BE PRESENT, BE RESPONSIBLE, BE ACCOUNTABLE."

To sum up my experience in Los Angeles: I met Ryan, I never once got shot, and I made plenty of friends.

It was hard work, but it was also incredibly fabulous and enriching. I feel fortunate that I got to play a tiny part in a huge and fascinating industry, and I love that I can still work there and visit as often as I can.

But the Hollywood years make up just a part of my writing career. I didn't particularly set out to interview celebrities, but I gravitated towards entertainment and showbusiness. Starting out on a local paper, and then teen mags, showed me a world that was a million miles away from life in a small seaside town. Pop music and mags like *Smash Hits* and *Just Seventeen* steered me through my teenage years. Looking back, it's no wonder I ended up where I did.

In my parallel life I always I thought I would end up being a war correspondent like Kate Adie or a political reporter covering Washington. I did neither but Hollywood and showbiz can sometimes be a war zone and there's plenty of politics so maybe in some weird way I achieved my goal?

But to set out on a career in journalism now is more than about goals. It's about staying power and tenacity.

When I was in my teens, there were plenty of opportunities for people like me – with no money and no Oxbridge credentials – to get a foot on the ladder. Local papers had training schemes that meant I could earn a good, living wage as I learnt how to do the job. It seems to me that the way people are paid in this industry now means that only those who come from wealthy backgrounds can afford to make a living. How an editorial assistant lives on £70 a day in London is beyond me [this is an actual day rate I know an editorial assistant at this moment in time is being paid]. They can only be funded by the bank of Mum and Dad and have second or even third jobs. I'm thankful that wasn't the case in my day as there was no bank or connections. As a comparison: My first day rate on *Just Seventeen* magazine in 1990 was £75.

Hopefully you will find a way.

My careers 'advisor' at sixth form college almost had to stifle a laugh when I told her that I wanted to be a journalist. She dismissed it out of hand and suggested I take up secretarial work: "You'd be good at that." Well I probably would have been but that wasn't my plan. I didn't have the heart to tell that I'd already done work experience, organised by myself, on the *Evening Echo*, the smaller *Leigh Times* newspaper and at *Essex Radio*.

Today it's less about work experience in the traditional sense and more about blogging, podcasting, and showing what you can do online.

Determination and focus counts for a lot but more than the financial aspect, it's been a tough time for journalists. It's never been particularly easy, but the Internet has shaken up the industry in a way that I imagine the advent of the printing press did in the 15th century.

Traditional media has found it hard to keep up with digital. I can only describe it as akin to being stranded on a desert island with someone you don't understand but have to find a way to live with in harmony.

Thankfully, a decade or more into this online revolution the two mediums are connecting and finding ways to co-exist and, dare I say it, support each other. I tell my students that print will never die and I mean it. Physical magazines and newspapers will always have an audience and there's nothing more satisfying than a beautifully written and researched long read. Also, celebrities will always want to be on the covers of magazines. They just can't help themselves. I do an entire lecture on this topic because I passionately believe it to be true.

If you've never bought a Sunday paper, I challenge you next weekend to buy one. Make breakfast, put some music on in the background, and spend a few hours reading it page by page. It's the most wonderful way to pass the time.

I'm not a total Luddite and appreciate being able to access news instantly on my phone. I'm used to it now, as are we all. But that wasn't always the case. When I lived in the Canary Islands for a short period of time in the early nineties, there were very few ways of keeping connected. The only English-speaking station I could receive was the BBC World Service, which was only really useful for news about the Congo. I'd write and receive physical letters from friends and family. Calls were made using handfuls of 100 peseta coins from a dusty phone box.

The British newspapers that arrived in the supermarkets were always two or three days old. I used to order the *Independent on Sunday* from our local shop. It arrived on a Monday and cost me 500 pesetas. That worked out about £3 which was a huge sum considering it cost just 60p back in the UK. In 1991 500 pesetas could fill up your petrol tank for the week. Mondays were my favourite day and I would have paid double for the thrill of being able to read a Sunday paper so far from home.

It's not just the changes in the industry a journalist has to deal with. There's the constant challenge of the perception of what you do and who you are. I talk in this book about never assuming anything. Many people outside of journalism assume they know it all about journalists without really knowing anything about us at all. The default setting appears to be that we're all liars, hackers, and sneaks. And don't get me started on the people who scream incessantly about 'fake news'. All that clap-trap has an effect. The general population are now wary of journalists. I've had people say things to me and then clamp their hands over their mouths as if I'm suddenly going to run to the nationals to sell whatever dreary nugget they've just imparted.

For the record, you're really not that interesting.

I've never gone through anyone's bin, hacked a phone, or tricked anyone into telling me anything they shouldn't. Journalism covers all areas. Lipstick, cars, travel, horses, advertising, cakes, movies, yachts, football. You get the idea. No one I know is putting out fake news. I'm not saying there aren't people with an agenda but it's just not normal practice for the average journo. The press absolutely should not be considered the enemy.

Press freedom is the bedrock of our democracy. That's why we have to be really good at what we do. Whether you're covering presidential elections, an innovation in waterproof mascara or the latest release on Netflix, you need to get your facts right. Most journalists I know are supremely hard working and now unfortunately horribly underpaid and having to work other jobs to keep doing what they love.

"Be present, be responsible, be accountable," is the title of this chapter and it's also a quote from Drew Barrymore. She used this phrase when I asked her how she runs her production company. It stuck with me because it helps to be all three in an industry which is under such scrutiny.

I've learnt a lot from interviewing celebrities. Mostly, that I like food too much to ever consider fame as an option, but also that living in a bubble isn't everything it's cracked up to be. I would urge you, though, to enjoy your time in the company of the rich and famous and be sure to eat as many snacks from hospitality as you can.

Everyone these days wants to be a celebrity, or so it seems, but having seen it at close quarters over so many years I'm not so sure it's the be all and end all. And we certainly shouldn't put these people on untouchable pedestals. Just because your face is pleasantly symmetrical doesn't mean you get to do what you like when you like.

So yes, I've learnt that people who look beautiful can be as irritating as they are charming, and also that persistence and hard work pays off as long as you have a good dollop of luck to go with it. You know what though, that's not just for celebrities, that goes for journalists too.

Persistence, talent, and hard work will take you far.

From Southend-on-Sea to Santa Monica, maybe?

So go forth and do your best. Use anything you've read here to do your job well or use none of it. There is no one way. You must forge your own path, fill your own toolbox, and rely on your own instincts.

These are my experiences and my lessons, and it's been a privilege to share them with you. Believe it or not, I'm still learning, still questioning, and still exploring; that's the beauty of a life lived with a press pass clipped to your jacket. The bylines are merely the shiny cherry on top of a very delicious cake.

CHAPTER 20

THE MISSING CHAPTERS

There are two chapters that haven't made the final cut of *Ryan is Ready for You Now...* Writing is all about editing and I wanted to share with you what they were and why they're not in this version of the book.

The first chapter I removed was called 'From Wolf Whistle to Weinstein' and it outlined some of the more inappropriate experiences I've endured during my career. There aren't many and they were a long time ago when I was younger and a lot more naïve than I am now. I wrote the chapter at the height of the #metoo movement and it was intensely cathartic because they were stories I'd never shared before and they lead to many interesting conversations.

I may eventually publish the chapter as a stand-alone piece because my test panel of readers were interested to hear about the experiences. Some of them worked with me at the time and had no idea these things had happened. I just wasn't ready to share them for many reasons, one of them being I didn't want to lose out on jobs in case my male editors thought I wasn't able to handle myself.

I initially thought the chapter could be useful to those starting out who might find themselves in similar situations. I took a step back when a trusted friend told me she thought it might be off-putting to younger journalists. She had a point and I took it on-board but that's not the only reason it's been removed.

Ultimately, I felt strongly that it didn't fit with the tone of the book which I wanted to keep entertaining, educational, and positive about an industry that has taken a battering in recent years. It maybe has a place somewhere but not here and not now. Even taking into account the need for light and shade in writing, the chapter jarred. On balance, I feel that the industry has evolved beyond those scrappy days of yore.

As you've hopefully gleaned from previous chapters, I don't believe that micro-managing is always a good thing but with such oversight today the chances of anyone finding themselves in the same situations as I did back in the day will probably not be repeated. Also, sitting here in the middle of pandemic I reckon the closest anyone will get to a celebrity for the foreseeable future is by touching the screen during a Zoom call. I very much hope the situation changes soon and that people around the world can start interacting again in person, and with all the beautiful freedoms we previously took for granted.

The second chapter I removed was the last in the book and was called ‘My Celebrity Wish List’.

Constantly updating it over the three years it’s taken me to write this lengthy tome I eventually realised that the chapter was never going to be fully formed or completed. It was in constant edit. And who am I kidding, if anyone commissions me to interview a celebrity, I’ll do it no matter who it is. I want to interview everyone. That’s the fun of being a writer in need of a commission and also a human who is incredibly nosy. I may upload it as a blog post on my website (www.lisamarksmedia.com) so that you can have a good chuckle or nod sagely and say, ‘Well, who wouldn’t want to interview Beyoncé on her yacht in the Med?’

Of course, there were some obvious choices in there so I’ll share a handful. In no particular order...

Donny Osmond if only to find out if he ever saw Southend Pier, and if not, does he want to bring the story full circle and visit now? This is a good a time as any as the pier hasn’t been set on fire or crushed by a tanker in years. I also want to apologise in person for thinking that he was so old, which he most definitely is now but then again, so am I, so we’re even.

And while I'm at it, let's give Bruce Willis another run up the flagpole. I'll be on my best behaviour and promise to ask actual questions this time. Keanu Reeves so that I can get a nose hair update.

I'd also really like to revisit Janice Dickinson. She's remarried and in a new phase of her life. I just know she has some more interesting stories to tell.

Charlize Theron but not at a junket. We're now beyond that. She can invite me to her home and that way she can curse at my face without causing a publicist to have a minor coronary. I enjoyed sparring with her so basically Charlize just for the fun of it.

Special shout out to Kermit the Frog because he's my hero and you know what, there's no connection without a rainbow connection. Hey, The Jim Henson Company, and some cool publication, get in touch!

And finally, Ryan Gosling.

We only had five minutes together.

He wore a Christmas jumper.

I wore the unpleasant sheen of a light sweat.

It's time to put that right, surely?

ACKNOWLEDGMENTS

Just like Kate Beckinsale, my own village is big. I've had a lot of help from some wonderful people. These are not just any old thank yous. If you're here, you've done above and beyond, and I love you with all my heart.

Kirstin Chaplin for so much I'd need another book but mostly for putting up with my daily musings and mitherings. Love you, sista. Chins up!

Sandy Bean (SBJQ) for her unwavering support, friendship, and endless enthusiasm. You have literally been a life saver and I love you to bits.

Laura Hills, who wore many hats, including that of unofficial editor and sounding board, as well as Destiny's Child playlist curator and provider of excellent coffee.

Genius stylist Henny Letailleur for her incredible talent, the laughs, and much appreciated supply of outfits and handbags. ("I don't understand").

Thank you, Nick Chalmers for the cover concept and cover design, and also to Danny Ledger for his design expertise.

The eagle-eyed, and always grammatically correct, Zoë Hill for enthusiastically proofreading this book like the champ that you are.

My friends and journalists who agreed to be quoted in this book: Kirstin Chaplin (two mentions!), Melissa Field, Joanne Hawkins (*Hello, BIG!*) and the singularly wonderful Julie Seddon, my mentor and dear friend and the one who has followed this journey 'from modest beginnings'. I simply cannot thank you enough.

High fives to both Kirsty Hatcher and James White. And thank you also to all the other journalists and publicists mentioned within these pages who I don't know personally but whose work has stayed with me, with special mentions to Alexandra Shakespeare and Catherine Shoard for their unwavering support over the years.

The inspirational and always impressive Ruth Elliott for appearing like an angel just when I needed her. Thank you, Ruthie.

Never-ending hugs for Craigy & Freddie, Phaedra, Jim, James & O-bags, Alex, Megan & Claudia, Margot, Rob & Jett, Ashley, Frankie & Lloyd, Chris G, Toby & Ross, Mark, Kate, Anne Marie, Sue, Emma, Aunty E, Tascha, Jessie, Toby & Emma, Vicky H, Lisa A, Trudie, Eileen, Kat and Jason, Sara, Claudie, & Nellie.

People talk about the teachers who inspired them and so I want to thank the late Peggy Batchelor and Hilary Wilson, respectively my head teacher and form teacher from Ridley. My education started on such a beautifully creative note there was no way life was ever going to be dull.

And finally – the big finish, the fireworks, and the champagne corks – my mum Babs and my brother Simon for always believing in me. You're both absolute-loo gorgeous.

ABOUT THE AUTHOR

Lisa Marks began her career as a journalist on the *Southend Evening Echo* at the age of 18. She freelanced for teen mags including *Just Seventeen* and *BIG!* before launching *Now* magazine in 1996 as showbiz editor. She went on to become a commissioning editor for the *Daily Mirror* and a reporter for *Media Guardian* before relocating to Los Angeles in 2007. In Hollywood, she wrote about the film, entertainment, and culture scene and her weekly LA Diary was published on *The Guardian* film blog. Covering the movie junket circuit, she also wrote celebrity profiles for *The Scotsman*, *Grazia*, *Red,* and *Sunday Magazine* (for the *Sunday Telegraph* in Sydney and the *Sunday Herald-Sun*).

Lisa has also written extensively for both the women's weekly and monthly markets and has lectured in journalism and magazine publishing at the University of Gloucester, Oxford Brookes University, and the University of Winchester. Her roast chicken is pretty impressive too.

If you've enjoyed this book and have a few pennies to spare I urge you to visit www.daughtersofcambodia.org who work to change lives for victims of human trafficking. Thank you.

The author looking very pleased with herself after her interview with Hugh Jackman at the Four Seasons Beverly Hills, in 2011.

Printed in Great Britain
by Amazon

72325339R00222